YO-CZP-599

What Others Have Said About

KidSpiration

"Bev and Judy have captured the essence of childhood ... the charm, the wonder, the fun. Over 200 stories, and every one is true. 'Kids do say the darndest things' ... just ask Art Linkletter. *KidsSpiration* is an idea whose time has come ... again!" —**Cavett Robert, CSP, CPAE**
Founder and Chairman Emeritus,
National Speakers Association

"This book contains great wisdom, hilarious humor, marvelous insights, and brutal honesty. Oh, to have such wonderful naivety and simple faith. The miracle of little ones lives in each of us. This book shows how we can let the miracle out and spread the love."
—**Robert Henry, CSP, CPAE**
Past President of National Speakers Association
Winner of the Cavett, the highest award
in professional speaking

"Children are the world's best educators and humorists. This delightful book captures their wisdom and wit. Must reading for those who want to laugh, learn and remember when." —**Dr. Charles V. Petty**
President, Family Success Unlimited
Nationally known family humorist

"*KidSpiration* ... *Out of the Mouths of Babes* ... a refreshing, delightful retreat for the soul, laughter and tears for the heart, and wisdom beyond adult fabrication. Treat yourself to the realness of life through kids' eyes and experience." —**Naomi Rhode, CSP, CPAE, Author**
Past President, National Speakers' Association

"As I turned the pages of *KidSpiration*, I found myself laughing out loud at the incredible, unpredictable, wonderful, spontaneous lines that could only come from children. This is a great book for anyone needing a good lift or a good laugh." —**Michael LeBoeuf, Ph.D.**
Author, *How to Win Customers and Keep Them for Life*
and *The Perfect Business*

"There are no greater treasures than our children, and their words are often jewels for our souls."

—**Barbara Hemphill**
Author, *Taming the Paper Tiger*

"Children are so honest! As I read these stories, I was reminded of several similar ones I've heard at my home and office. This recollection, which will probably occur to most readers, adds to the value and pleasure of the book."

—**Robert L. Abney III, M.D.**
Pediatritian, Children's Medical Group

"Tom T. Hall wrote that '... old dogs care about you even when you make a mistake, and little children while they're still too young to hate.' This book quotes children before they learn from some sorry adult how to hate. I recommend this book. It brings back precious memories about *my* children."

—**Jerry Clower**
Humorist and Author
Member, Grand Ole Opry
MCA Recording Artist

"What a spectacular way to build a healthy generation! This book, along with the *KidSpirational Keepsakes Journal,* are sure-fire ways to strengthen families and affirm self-esteem for a lifetime."

—**Patty Hendrickson**
Professional Speaker, specializing in
Self-Esteem for Students

"These wonderful stories will inspire everyone to think and reflect upon the many delightful experiences of children. An essential book for the young and old alike."

—**Dr. Frances A. Karnes**
Author, *Girls* and *Young Women Lead the Way*
Director, Center for Gifted Studies,
University of Southern Mississippi

"This book will lift your spirit into the heavenlies and tickle your funny bone. Best of all, it will provide you with the enthusiasm for a 'Fresh Start' with your own children and grandchildren!"

—**Glenna Salsbury, CSP, CPAE**
President, National Speakers Association, 1997
Author, *The Art of the Fresh Start*

KidSpiration

Out of the Mouths of Babes

Judy Moon Denson
AND
Beverly Smallwood, Ph.D

ILLUSTRATED BY
Kym Garraway

FOREWORD BY
Art Linkletter

QUAIL RIDGE PRESS

Copyright © 1997 by
Judy Moon Denson and Beverly Smallwood

ISBN 0-937552-86-0

All rights reserved

Printed in the United States of America

No part of this book may be reproduced or utilized in any form or by any means, electronic or mechanical, including photocopying and recording, or by any information storage and retrieval system, without permission in writing from the publisher.

Library of Congress Cataloging-in-Publication Data

Denson, Judy Moon
    KidSpiration--Out of the Mouths of Babes / Judy Moon Denson and Beverly Smallwood; illustrated by Kym Garraway; foreword by Art Linkletter.
        p. cm.
    Includes index.
    ISBN 0-937552-86-0 (alk. pper)
    1. Children--Quotations. 2. Children--Humor. I. Smallwood, Beverly. II. Title.
PN6328.C5D45 1997
305.23--dc21   97-2935
                                           CIP

Published by
QUAIL RIDGE PRESS
P. O. Box 123 · Brandon, MS 39043
1-800-343-1583

Lovingly Dedicated to Our Children
Jill and Molly, Greg and Amy

They come from every corner of the globe
. . . your kids and my kids.
Boys and girls just waiting to "explode!"
. . . we really like kids.
When cultures, creeds, and colors blend
like rainbows do . . .
It's celebrational! . . .
They're KidSpirational—Kids!

Excerpt from theme song, "KidSpirational Kids"

Contents

Acknowledgments

KidSpiration has been a team effort. We give applause, salutes, blessings, hugs, and thanks to our teammates, coaches, and cheerleaders.

- To our husbands, Hill and Fred . . . for their patience, support, and encouragement in generous amounts.
- To our mothers, Merle Moon and Wilma Hannaford . . . for believing in us, as always.
- To Lezlee Welch . . . for countless hours invested in manuscript production, editing, organization, and documentation . . . and for not resigning when we re-wrote the book for the thirtieth time!
- To Jill Denson Thomas and Virginia Lawless . . . for their valuable clerical and emotional support.
- To Maggie Williams, freelance writer, who gave the concept of the book its first print exposure.
- To Dan Sullivan, The Strategic Coach©, who helped sharpen the focus on unique abilities and new capabilities.
- To Glenna Salsbury, Bev's mentor, role model, and cherished friend.
- To those who read the manuscript and provided the endorsements that appear on the cover and front pages.
- To Kym Garraway, our talented illustrator and dear friend.
- To Joseph Britain . . . for applying his musical genius to the arrangement of our theme song, "KidSpirational Kids."
- To our special encouragers: Kate Andrews, Linda Bell, Christine Belleris, Dianna Booher, Jennifer Borislow, Bertha Bunda, Jim Cameron, James Ducker, Jennifer Enderlin, Liz Higgs, Billy Hudson, Georgia Hughes, Willie Jolley, Art May, Byron McCauley, Mike McPhail, Gene Owens, Freeman Parker, Dennis Polk, Tandy Rice, Cavett Robert, Betsy Rowell, Kelly Sanner, Kathy Stogner, George Walther, Jon Mark Weathers, and Nina Woolverton.
- To WDAM-TV, *The Hattiesburg American*, and *The Mississippi Business Journal*, who treated our vision for the book as a "done deal."
- To our publishers, Quail Ridge Press . . . especially Barney, Gwen, and Shawn McKee . . . for embracing us as family, for sharing with us the magic of book creation, and for helping make our dream a reality.

We love you all!

Foreword

"During my 60-year broadcasting career, the high-light of my professional efforts involved talking to children of 4 to 10 years of age: 5 days a week, 52 weeks a year, for 26 years. I explored the minds of the little ones on an un-rehearsed basis resulting in my book *Kids Say the Darndest Things* which went on to become the [#]1 non-fiction best seller for two years.

Now Beverly and Judy have stumbled across this gold mine of original humor and I congratulate them on this delightful collection, *KidSpiration,* that is truly out of the mouths of babes.

I predict that everyone who reads this will find something to chuckle about, something to ruminate about, and something that will recall a delightful moment in one's own family life.

Art Linkletter
Author, *Kids Say the Darndest Things*

Introduction

"Children grow up while we're not looking." That little quote made me sentimental even when my children were still years away from leaving home. I sensed that one day I would look back with longing.

In our "busyness" today, some of us remember the home of our childhood as a place where life slowly unfolded—at the kitchen sink doing dishes, curling up in our mother's lap to hear a story with a creaky rocker marking time, or shelling peas under a shade tree on a warm summer day.

I grew up knowing that one day I would earn a degree. And have a career. And have a family. But how could I have known that in all my striving, my heart and head would play tricks on each other. At work, my heart drifted toward home. When I was at home, a voice inside my head said, "Did you forget to do something at the office?"

I'm sure that many young mothers are caught up in that same balancing act. I feel for them and for the children they love, because it is clear to me now—kids are not kids very long. When childhood is gone, it doesn't come back. That's reason enough not to miss it!

When my daughters began to speak in phrases, I started journals for them. I wanted to save their words and chronicle their earliest attempts to interpret the world—a baffling place, a dwelling they had entered through no choice of their own.

"Read me what I said, Mama," Jill would say, as she climbed onto my lap holding her book. In time, my second child, Molly, would do the same with her book. This gave us a chance to reflect on how precious each child was, and also to appreciate how they had progressed.

While it was my job to get it all down in story form, the girls' daddy was the one who kept me on track. He would say, "Baby, you need to write that one down." (Never mind the flour up to my elbows or the burgers burning on the stove.)

Even with the help of my sweet mother who lives with us, it was very difficult to stop long enough to write down "who said what." But it was worth the effort! My children's books mean more to us than anything else we own. And Dr. Beverly Smallwood, co-creator of *KidSpiration*, assures me that these simple acts helped my daughters develop a sense of self early in life.

So, was life always wonderful at our house? Definitely not! We struggled just like other families, but that's the reason this matters so much. All families need a little laughter to balance the other stuff, something warm and genuine, a chance to be present in the moment—just for the joy of it.

Writing this book and reliving our early years as a family has been a spiritual experience for me; in essence, a healing. I hope you will be inspired to start a journal for your own children—and grandchildren! You can be the one to start a tradition, to preserve the unique flavor of your own family for generations to come, to let them know what life was like back in the "good ole days"—the '90s and beyond!

What was it that first caught my attention? It was *The Belly Button Theory of Creation*, contributed by Jill, my first born, who has always had a fascination with things celestial.

Judy Moon Denson

The Belly Button
Theory of Creation

Jill, Age 3
Daughter of Judy Moon Denson

Jill was giving Molly, her brand new baby sister, the "once-over." Spotting Molly's navel, she asked, "What's THAT?"

"That's where the baby was connected to her mother before she was born," her mom explained. "It's called a belly button. Everybody has one."

Jill replied, "Everybody has a belly button, except God!"

"In the beginning—God!"
Child-like faith . . . so innocent, so beautiful. Believing came easy for Jill. Her mind was still fresh and open, unlike many of us who have been left jaded by the harsh experiences of life.
At the age of three, Jill knew. God came first, and out of that Love came all creation.
And so it is that we are all connected. God's love flows through us and out to others.
As you read and reflect on the stories that follow allow them to bring refreshment, renewal, laughter, and maybe even a brand new beginning!

Ins and Outs

Molly, Age 7
Daughter of Judy Moon Denson

Molly had spent the afternoon with her friend, Shannon. When she got home, she threw the back door open and ran to her mother.

"Look, Mom!" she exclaimed, holding out her tiny palm. "Shannon's dad gave me 50 cents, and he gave her 50 cents, too!"

"Really?" her mother responded.

"Yes," Molly continued. "We had a puppet show!"

Mom played along. "And you made him pay to get in?"

She said, "No . . . to get out!"

Most things in life are easier to get into than to get out of—and usually there is a price to be paid!

Divine Calling

Bill, Age 7

Bill's parents were going next door to play bridge with the neighbors. Bill would be staying home alone . . . against his wishes.

"We'll be right next door," they assured him. "Now, we don't want the phone ringing every five minutes, Bill. But if you really need us, call us." And they left.

They had no more than sat down to the bridge game when the phone rang. Predictably, it was Bill.

"Mama, I'm so lonesome," he said, "What's the number for Dial-a-Prayer?"

I probably deserve the medal for loneliness . . .
but who would think of nominating me?
ASHLEIGH BRILLIANT
Pot-Shots epigrams by Ashleigh Brilliant
of Santa Barbara, CA, appear by special permission

This is the Life

Kelly, Age 5

"What do you want to be when you grow up?" Kelly's kindergarten teacher asked. "A doctor? A lawyer? Or an astronaut maybe?"

This was virgin territory for Kelly, and the answer would take some time.

Later that week, Kelly and her stay-at-home mom were into their afternoon ritual—sitting on the floor in front of the television, munching snacks and talking.

Suddenly Kelly had a revelation, "I've got it!" she said, looking at her mother through eyes of love. "When I grow up, I want to be a nobody just like you."

*There are those among us who see motherhood as something more than a job—a **calling**. Kelly's mom accepted the call, and thanks to sufficient financial resources, she was able to set aside personal pursuits and take "time out" to be with her children.*

Time, after all, is a vital component in bringing up our little ones—time for taking a leisurely stroll—time to stop and pick up pretty rocks—time to listen to the wind in the trees.

*Kelly's mom—a nobody? No. Rather, a **somebody** with **no title**, except for the one that mattered most to both of them—MOTHER.*

Ring My Chimes

Garrett, Age 4

Theirs was a busy household, made up of a dad, a mom, and two active pre-schoolers. Mom occasionally retreated to the bathroom to have a little time just for herself.

The kids understood that when she went in there, they were not to bother her except in an emergency.

One evening, just after going into her sanctuary, she heard a knock on the door.

"Who is it?" she asked.

"Garrett," he confessed sheepishly.

"I need a little time to myself, Garrett. You can't come in," she said firmly.

Seconds later, there was another knock. By now, she was irritated, knowing it was Garrett again.

"Who is it?" she asked, her tone practically daring the would-be intruder to identify himself.

Thinking fast and hoping for a better outcome this time, he answered, "Pizza guy."

If you only knock long enough and loud enough at the gate, you are sure to wake up somebody.
HENRY WADSWORTH LONGFELLOW

Safety First

Drew, Age 4
Son of Patti Hathaway, CSP
Professional Speaker
Author, *Giving and Receiving Criticism* and *Managing Upward*

Drew and his dad were riding in the car when Drew noticed a squirrel in the middle of the road. The squirrel had obviously met its demise.

"Daddy, is that a squirrel?" Drew inquired.

"Yes," said his dad.

"Is he dead?" Drew said in a quieter voice.

"Yes, he is, Drew."

Thoughtfully, Drew concluded, "He must not have looked both ways."

I Want it Now!

Katy Clower, Age 6
Daughter of Jerry Clower, Humorist and MCA Recording Artist

The Clower clan motored down the interstate. Little Katy was lying peacefully on the back seat, watching billboards zoom past the window, including one with a full-color picture of Colonel Sanders and his Kentucky Fried Chicken. It was more than Katy could stand.

Suddenly, she bolted up, shouting, "Daddy! Stop the car! Stop the car!"

"Katy, what on earth is the matter?" Jerry asked, matching her urgency.

"You GOTTA pull over, Daddy," she pleaded. "Colonel Sanders done flung a cravin' on me!"

Necks of Kin

Amy, Age 5

A steady stream of visitors poured into the hospital to see the new baby. Amy, getting into the big sister role, directed traffic to the nursery.

By the time her aunt arrived, Amy had studied the baby in some detail, stem to stern.

"Don't worry, Aunt Ruth," she said with authority. "He'll grow a neck."

Hum A Few Bars

Scott, Age 6

Scott had become increasingly frustrated during the song service at church. He couldn't read, and he didn't have the words of the hymns memorized, so he couldn't sing along.

One Sunday after church, Scott tugged on the pastor's sleeve.

"Dr. Turner, I don't like the songs y'all sing in church," Scott complained. "I don't know the words."

"I'm sorry about that, Scott," the pastor replied. "Maybe you could suggest a song that you do know the words to, and we could sing that one next Sunday."

"Great!" Scott answered. "Let's sing, 'I Got Friends in Low Places'!"

Listen Up!

Richard, Age 6

It had been a trying Monday in Ms. Hannaford's first grade classroom. Richard, a difficult student, had traced the teacher's steps throughout the day, tugging at her skirt and calling her name repeatedly.

Normally extremely patient, she had reached her limit! She took him into the hall and lectured him sternly.

"Richard, you follow me everywhere, you don't listen to me, and you don't follow the rules. You MUST sit down and do your work!"

As she spoke, Richard listened, wide-eyed. She began to feel guilty for being so harsh. After all, Richard did have some problems. Maybe she had damaged his self esteem.

Before she could finish the thought, Richard broke the silence. "Ms. Hannaford, you've got white teeth just like my dog!"

Ms. Wilma Hannaford is my mother . . . a model of kindness, encouragement, and support. She gave me both roots and wings. She was always there, always ready to "listen up" when I needed an ear. Thanks, Mom.
BEVERLY SMALLWOOD

Ain't Misbehavin'

Richard, Age 10

It had been quite a day. Richard and his older brother Harry had chosen to challenge authority repeatedly, and therefore, had suffered the consequences. Their parents, in a united front, applied appropriate measures to reinforce and reestablish the rules, no easy task!

When bedtime came, the boys said their prayers as usual. Richard with his "halo" firmly in place, closed by saying, "And Lord, please forgive *Mama and Daddy* of their many sins!"

I-O-U, U-O-ME

Lillian, Age 5
Daughter of Liz Curtis Higgs,
CSP, CPAE, An Encourager®
Author, Humorist, Professional Speaker

One May day, Lillian said to her mother, "What are you getting me for Mother's Day?"

"Darling," her mother said, "this is the one day of the year stuff is supposed to flow in *my* direction!"

Hands on her hips, Lillian said, "Well! You wouldn't even *be* a mother if it weren't for me!"

Excerpt from *Only Angels Can Wing It, The Rest of Us Have to Practice.* Thomas Nelson, Publisher. 1995. Used with permission.

Dinner is Served

Nichole, Age 3

Nichole was excited about seeing the neighbor's new baby for the first time.

When she went to visit, the baby was contentedly nursing at its mother's breast. Naturally Nichole was curious about the procedure, never having witnessed anything quite like it.

The baby's mother attempted to explain it to Nichole the same way she had explained it to the baby's siblings.

"Nichole," she said, "this baby does not drink milk from a bottle." Nichole still looked puzzled. The explanation expanded. "Have you ever seen puppies eat?"

Nichole nodded yes.

"Well, that's how I feed the baby."

Horrified, she responded, "Out of a bowl on the floor?"

Divine Intervention

Mark, Age 4

Mark was misbehaving in church service. His mother hated to take him outside. She knew it would be a distraction to his grandfather, who just happened to be the preacher.

Things went from bad to worse and she knew—in fact, *everyone* knew—she had no choice.

She rose to her feet, picked him up, and moved quickly down the aisle toward the door. Suddenly the gravity of the situation hit the boy, and he called back to the congregation, pleading, "Won't *somebody* please pray!"

Boxed In

Andrew, Age 5

Andrew had never been to a funeral home. Before going inside, his parents did their best to prepare him for the experience.

"Stay right with me, Andrew," his mother said. "Hold my hand, and use your quiet voice. We won't stay long, OK?"

Andrew's mom was soon lost in somber conversation. Suddenly she became aware that he was no longer holding her hand. She did a quick scan of the parlor and saw him walking toward the coffin. At that very moment, Andrew spotted his dad on the other side of the room, caught up in the crowd.

"HEY, DAD!" he yelled, "WHO'S THE MAN IN THE BOX?"

Think out of the box!   MIKE VANCE

... Or Two or Three

Robby, Age 4

Robby had the floor at the family dinner table. He waxed eloquent, explaining to his parents why Jesus had died on the cross. Further, he "enlightened" his parents with an elaborate description of what sin was all about.

"How do you know so much about sin?" his mom asked.

Robby replied, "Because I done one!"

Never regret and never look back. Regret is an appalling waste of energy. You can't build on it; it's only good for wallowing in.   UNKNOWN

You know, by the time you reach my age, you've made plenty of mistakes, and if you've lived your life properly, you learn. You put things in perspective. You pull your energies together. You change. You go forward.   RONALD REAGAN

A Rose By Any Other Name

Jill, Age 9
Daughter of Judy Moon Denson

Jill and her fifth-grade class were excited about their field trip. It would give them a first-hand look at some of the plants they had studied in science. When the day finally arrived, Jill's mom went along as a chaperone.

The walking trail carried them deep into the woods. Jill's mother pointed out various plants and called them by name, and Jill was pleased that her mother knew so much.

"Oh, my mom has lots of plants," Jill said to her classmates, beaming, "nasturtiums, marigolds, *dogonias . . .*"

Zip Your Lip

Shobie, Age 5

Shobie was talking nonstop as he and his mom headed home on the rapid transit system. A couple sitting behind him couldn't help overhearing when he said something amusing, and they laughed.

Shobie didn't like that a bit because he thought they were laughing *at* him. And so, he stuck his tongue out at them.

His mother whispered in his ear, "Shobie, I'd rather you kept your tongue in your mouth during train rides."

"Why?" he asked loudly. "Is our tongue one of our private parts?"

You can tame a tiger, but you can't tame a tongue.
James 3:8 *The Message*

Parts is Parts

Melody, Age 6

Ms. Tamberg asked her Monday morning first grade class, "What did you do for fun this weekend?"

Melody spoke up, "I went to the zoo with my mama and daddy."

"Really?" her teacher said. "Did your brothers and sisters go with you?"

"No, ma'am," Melody answered. "I don't have any brothers and sisters. In fact, my mama can't have any more children . . . she had her tonsils out!"

Northern Exposure

Sam, Age 6

Sam walked into the bedroom unexpectedly as his mother was in the process of getting dressed.

Pointing to her chest, Sam asked with genuine interest, "Mom, has Dad seen those?"

Gripper Zipper

Randy, Age 7

The second-grade teacher had granted Randy permission to leave class to go to the rest room. When he did not return in a timely manner, she became concerned and sent John to check on him. More time passed, and John didn't come back either.

Finally, she sent Jerry to check on his buddies. Jerry did return, but the news was not good.

"Ms. Beck," he said, shaking his head, "Randy won't be coming back any time soon. He's got his kidneys hung in his zipper!"

*Caught in a bind: no matter which way you move, more pain is inevitable! There are no **good** choices, just some that are slightly less distressing than others. Often, we also have to admit that **we** "pulled up the zipper!"*

When a personal bind has you stuck, unable to move . . . recognize that the past cannot be changed; learn from it, and let it go; stop focusing on "what if," and begin to make use of "what is!"

Life Cycles

Amy, Age 5

The Sunday school teacher always started the class with prayer, and she enjoyed giving the children a chance to be involved.

"Now, boys and girls . . . is there anyone we need to pray for . . . perhaps a friend or a family member?" she asked.

Amy spoke up. "Yes, pray that my mom won't have PMS."

Well, Purple *Is* a Royal Color!

Elise, Age 2

Elise sat proudly in "big church" with her parents during the special Christmas service. Elise especially loved the carols, and she sang along with the ones she knew.

"*Noel, Noel . . . ,*" they sang.

She wasn't so familiar with that one, so she listened attentively to catch the words.

"*. . . Noel, Noel. Born is the King of Is-ra-el!*"

Elise's mouth and eyes flew open wide and her voice rang out through the church:

"*BARNEY'S* the King of Is-ra-el???"

Time Will Tell

Jessica, Age 4

"So, what happened at kindergarten today?" Jessica's mom asked.

"Ryan asked me if I would marry him when we grow up," she said matter-of-factly.

"What did you tell him?" her mother asked.

"I told him I would have to think about it," she said seriously. "I might have some other offers."

Face Value

Rachel, Age 4

Rachel made a "not-so-nice" comment. Her mother corrected her both verbally and visually. In fact, the look of disapproval lasted for quite a while after the exchange.

Finally, Rachel said, "I *am* sorry, Mommy. Now can you get rid of your mad face?"

If you're happy, notify your face.   UNKNOWN

Laughter is the sun that drives winter from the human face.   VICTOR HUGO

Message From Above

Tyler, Age 5

The first day of kindergarten was finally over. All the children would be riding the bus home except for Tyler. His mother would pick him up.

"Just stay in the classroom, Tyler. I'll be right back," the teacher said as she left to take the other children to the bus. As the teacher walked past the office, she asked Mr. Carr, the principal, to check on Tyler.

Instead of going to the room, he decided to use the intercom, a system that was brand new to Tyler. In a clear, booming voice, Mr. Carr called out, "Tyler?"

There was no answer.

Louder this time, he asked, "Tyler, are you there?"

A tiny, trembling, submissive voice answered the call. "Yes, God, I am."

*Ever think God is calling your name? At times, you may have sensed that you were being called to do something, but you dismissed the feeling, or you doubted your ability to do it. Time **alone** can permit the still, small voice within us to come through "loud and clear."*

God can do anything, you know—far more than you could ever imagine or guess or request in your wildest dreams! He does it not by pushing us around but by working within us, His Spirit deeply and gently within us. THE APOSTLE PAUL, Ephesians 3:20, The Message

One of *THEM*

Erin, Age 8
Mallory, Age 12

As the 1996 Presidential election approached, Erin and her sister Mallory had lots of questions for their Republican parents.

Mallory wanted to know the difference between a Republican and a Democrat.

Her mother explained, "Well, Republicans believe in not wasting the country's money. Democrats seem to want to spend money for all the things they want."

Startled, Erin threw her hands in the air and yelled, "Oh, my Lordy, Mama, I think I'm a Democrat!"

Fresh Squeezed

Emily, Age 3

Emily walked into the bedroom just in time to see her mom nursing the new baby. Emily climbed onto the bed, sat cross-legged, and studied the scene carefully. Finally, Emily pointed to where the baby was nursing and asked, "What's that?"

"That's where the baby gets its milk," her mother replied.

After a while, her mom moved the baby to the other side to continue the feeding.

Emily inquired, "So . . . what's that? Juice?"

Like Magic

Jill, Age 4
Daughter of Judy Moon Denson

Mom and Dad were determined . . . Jill needed to learn to say "please" and "thank you." Most of the time she remembered, but one morning she forgot.

"Get me some apple juice," she demanded flatly.

Obviously, this was one of those times she needed to be reminded, so her mother prompted, "What's the magic word?"

Without hesitating, Jill said, "Abracadabra!"

Wiggle Room

Avery, Age 2

Avery was riding along with his Aunt Lezlee and his cousin, Dustin.

"I had a goldfish," he said, "but I ate it."

"You *ate* it?" his aunt asked.

"Yep," he said, "and it wiggled going down!"

It's Not Over Til It's Over

Dallas, Age 4

The game between the San Diego Aztecs and the Wyoming Cowboys had been a roller coaster ride. The crowd went wild as the lead was passed back and forth between the two teams. Little Dallas, attending the game with his grandmother, was having a ball.

Then, two minutes before the clock ran out, the Aztecs made a touchdown, giving them a one-point lead. The Aztec fans, including Dallas and Grandma Kate, were on their feet, clapping and cheering as the clock ran out.

"Yeah! It's over! We won!" Grandma yelled.

Dallas started crying, even more loudly than everyone else was cheering.

"No, it's not over!" he insisted.

"Yes, Dallas, it's over! We won!"

Dallas was inconsolable. He cried even harder, as his grandma swept him up and away from staring eyes and toward the exit.

"NO! NO! It's NOT over!" he protested. *"The fat lady didn't sing!"*

Just You Wait!

Christina, Age 6
Trevor, Age 4

Christina and her 4-year-old brother Trevor, were making a Saturday afternoon trip to Dairy Queen with their grandfather.

Trevor said suddenly, "I'm really sexy!"

"Trevor! Don't say that!" his sister scolded. "That's a bad word!"

Trevor wasn't convinced. "That's not a bad word, is it, Pa-Paw?"

"Well," his grandfather hesitated, "it's not really a *bad* word. I guess you could say it's an *adult* word."

Determined to make her point, Christina added, "Well, I'll say one thing, Trevor. If you knew what that word really meant, you'd NEVER say it again in your whole life!"

Today's children are required to learn what most people in former times were forbidden to know.

ASHLEIGH BRILLIANT
Pot-Shots epigrams by Ashleigh Brilliant of
of Santa Barbara, CA, appear by special permission

Cutting Edge

B.J., Age 5

It was a lively family discussion. Mom, Dad, Bryant, and B.J. were talking about plans for another baby . . . hopefully, a girl this time.

B.J. said, "If you want a baby boy, your daddy has to go to the hospital and get him, and your mother has to go to the hospital if it's a girl."

Fascinated with his theory, B.J.'s mother pressed him further. "B.J., how do they get the baby out of the mother's tummy?"

B.J. thought for a moment, then answered, "Well, they would have to use a real sharp knife or a pizza cutter!"

"We Deliver."

Internal Combustion

Kelsey, Age 4

There was quite a lot of talk around the house about the baby that was growing in Mommy's "tummy." One morning, Mom was brushing Kelsey's hair, standing right behind her.

Suddenly her mom's stomach growled at close range to Kelsey's ears. Amazed and wide-eyed, she inquired, "Mom! What does that baby *do* in there?"

It's Contagious

Sara, Age 3

Sara watched as her mother downed a couple of aspirin tablets.

"Here, Sara, you want the rest of my water?" her mother said, offering her the glass.

"No," Sara said. "It has headaches in it."

No "Pwace" Like Home

Heather, Age 4

Michelle's first day away from her mother was tough. The teacher at The Yellow Brick Road Day Care Center had given her several chances to join the other kids. But Michelle kept going to the window, gazing down the street where her mom had gone.

Heather, a day care veteran, reached out and put her arm around Michelle. "Pwease don't cwy," Heather said tenderly. "You get usen to it."

CHANGE . . . do we ever "get usen to it?"

Change requires us to "leave home" . . . the place where we have become comfortable. It's very hard to let go of "what was" and "the way we were."

Yet some people actually thrive on change. Stress researchers have identified four "hardiness factors" that characterize flexible, resilient people.
- *They view change as a challenge.*
- *They commit to engage life, not avoid it.*
- *They have a clear sense of mission.*
- *They maintain a sense of control, refusing to "become victims."*

When you're through changing, you're through.
                                        BRUCE BARTON

All's Fair in Love and War

Lee, Age 7
Daughter of Cavett Robert, Founder and Chairman Emeritus
National Speakers Association

Hallie Cavett Robert, Lee's grandmother and the matriarch of the family, came to spend the winter in the Robert's Phoenix home. Hal, as they referred to her, was a great storyteller. She spent a couple of hours every morning with the children telling stories that were a combination of fiction and fact. As a result, the children didn't know until they went to school that the North had won the War Between the States, a small detail Hal had failed to mention!

Hal spoke of Robert E. Lee with great reverence, so much so that Lee finally asked, "Daddy, was Hal *married* to Robert E. Lee?"

She is a sweet ole Southern belle
Who never talks too fast;
She drawls her "y'alls" and "I declares"
And dreams about the past.

CHARLES GHIGNA

Miracle Cure

Aubrey, Age 4

Pastor Polk noticed a sad-faced Aubrey shuffling down the aisle after church. "What's wrong, Aubrey?" asked the pastor.

"I don't feel good," Aubrey explained. "My throat hurts, I got some fever, and I got a runny nose."

"I'm really sorry about that, Aubrey," the pastor said. "Would you like me to pray for you?"

"Yes, sir," Aubrey said.

Sitting down with the boy on the first pew, Pastor Polk took Aubrey by the hand and prayed an eloquent prayer for his recovery. When they opened their eyes, there was a period of silence.

Then Aubrey looked the pastor squarely in the eye and said, "I don't feel *NO BETTER!*"

The Miracle of Metamorphosis

Jakeman, Age 3

Jakeman was expressive by nature . . . lots of hand gestures with brows raised and eyes wide. That was his style from the time he started to talk.

When his mother came home from teaching school one day, the sitter told her what Jakeman had said to her and his younger brother, Jesse.

"Life is like a butterfly. You know how caterpillars are ugly and then turn beautiful? Well, that's what God does to us. We have an ugly heart, and he changes us to a beautiful person."

> *Create in me a clean heart, O God, and renew a right spirit within me.*   DAVID, Psalm 51:10

If You Don't Have A Dream

Jennifer, Age 7

When Jennifer was adopted by loving parents at age two, she was unable to walk, had a limited vocabulary, and was "emotionally disadvantaged." Even though she had come a long way by second grade, she remained painfully shy. She had to endure teasing by the other kids because of her thick glasses, "thick as a Coke bottle!"

Jennifer's teacher had noticed that the child showed an unusual interest in fairy tales, particularly the stories featuring blonde-haired, blue-eyed princesses. One day, Jennifer looked up through her chestnut-colored bangs at her blonde, blue-eyed teacher. She said, "Ms. Smith, you look like *you* could be a princess."

In fairy tales, princesses are physically beautiful. They have charm and grace. They have blonde hair and blue eyes. Implied in Melissa's statement is the belief that she herself could never qualify.

All of us need visions... hopes... dreams. Without them, we remain stuck where we are. With them, we move toward what matters most to us. Dreams challenge our minds and order our steps.

> *I have a dream.*   MARTIN LUTHER KING

> *Cherish your visions and your dreams, as they are the children of your soul; blueprints of your ultimate achievements.*   NAPOLEON HILL

47

Let's Party!

Lindsey and Lauren, Age 4

Tomorrow was to be the big day . . . the twins' birthday party. All weekend the family had labored to get the three-acre yard in tip-top shape . . . raking, mowing, planting, pruning . . . *the works!*

When the sun came up Sunday morning, they scurried to get out the door with all four children so they could make it to church on time. When Katie opened the door, she let out a scream.

Their beautiful yard was a mess! Pink and white toilet paper streamers adorned the huge pine trees. And all the shrubs. And most of the grass. The work of teenage pranksters!

Their mom was heart sick. "We worked so hard. How will we explain this to the twins?"

About that time, Lauren and Lindsey came running out the door. Then something wonderful happened. In the 'eyes of the beholders', the desecration was seen as decoration . . . for the party, of course! Lauren looked up at her dad with tears in her eyes, "Oh, Daddy, it's beautiful!" she said, hugging his leg.

Lindsey hugging his other leg said, "Daddy, this is going to be the best birthday party ever!"

Invisible Protective Shield

Jill, Age 9
Daughter of Judy Moon Denson

Jill was watching a television program with her mother. She walked to the TV set, and touching the screen, she said to her mom, "If this broke, we could touch the people, couldn't we?"

The following story appeared in newspapers across the country:

FATHER CHARGED WITH KILLING TODDLER FOR INTERRUPTING GAME

DALLAS (AP) — A 3-year-old boy died after his father punched him several times in the stomach for making noise during a televised Dallas Cowboys football game, police said.

A horror story... repeated symbolically on a daily basis.
"Sh-h-h! I can't hear! This is the big play!"
"Why do you always have to bring these things up in the middle of my favorite program?"
Maybe if television sets were turned off at intervals, we could re-discover the people who matter most, and find new ways to "touch" each other.

Mistaken Identity

Jill, Age 10
Daughter of Judy Moon Denson

Jill and her dad had just settled in for the afternoon football game on TV when the announcer said that Florida would be playing Brigham Young.

Jill wondered aloud, "Brigham Young—I've heard of him. Wasn't he the leader of the Morons?"

Clearly a case of mislabeling—words that only sound similar. Jill's remark was made in innocence. Some of the labels adults use are not. Labels limit love.

If you judge people, you have no time to love them.
MOTHER TERESA

Don't pick on people, jump on their failures, criticize their faults—unless, of course, you want the same treatment. That critical spirit has a way of boomeranging. JESUS CHRIST, *Matthew 7:1, The Message*

Close Connection

Scott, Age 6

One afternoon, Scott was playing in the front yard with the children from the neighborhood. Suddenly, he burst through the door calling his mom, who was expecting a baby. The group had a question, and he was the designated inquirer.

"Mama," he said, out of breath, "how does the baby eat in your stomach?"

His mother pulled a book off the shelf and showed him a picture of an unborn baby and explained how the umbilical cord provides nourishment.

Relieved, he went back to his friends.

"Well, I just want you to know . . . the baby can eat and drink just like us, because God put an extension cord in Mama's stomach."

It's a Beautiful Day in the Neighborhood

Andy, Age 6

Andy had been learning the Lord's Prayer in Sunday School.

Right before church Sunday morning, his mother asked him if he had it memorized.

"No, not really," he replied.

"Well, do you at least know the first line?" she asked.

"Ummm ... Our Father in heaven?" he guessed.

"That's a start," his dad said. "How about the second line?"

Andy thought for a minute, then said, "Hello, be my neighbor?"

Mountains vs. Molehills

J.B., Age 3

Quiet time at last! J.B.'s mom was relaxing in the tub, something she normally did in private. The door suddenly opened. It was J.B.

She took one look, pointed at her mother's modest chest, and exclaimed, "Elf ninnies!"

> *If you stick your chest out, somebody will come along and flatten it for you!*   UNKNOWN

Look Who's Talking

Ann, Age 5

When Ann misbehaved, her mother had a way of finding out . . . every time!

"*How does she do that?!*" Ann wondered.

Reading Ann's mind, her mother said, "A little bird told me."

Ann gritted her teeth and said, "I'm gonna **kill** that bird!"

> *So live that you wouldn't be ashamed to sell the family parrot to the town gossip.*   WILL ROGERS

Half & Half

Taylor, Age 2

What fun it was for Taylor and her mom to go through the bag of hand-me-downs that Taylor's aunt had just brought! When Taylor spotted swimsuits, she was ecstatic. She loved to play in the water.

As she began to pull the swimsuits out of the bag, she encountered her first "two-piece."

"Oh, shoot!" she complained. "It's bwoke!"

No, No, They Can't Take *THAT* Away!

Claire, Age 3

Claire went to the dentist's office with her 7-year-old sister Andrea and their mom. Claire perched on her mom's lap to watch as the dentist examined Andrea.

The dentist noticed out of the corner of his eye that Claire was sucking her thumb. "She shouldn't do that," he said to her mother. "It will make her teeth protrude, and she'll have to wear braces."

Later that evening, Claire came to her mom and asked very seriously, "Mommy, why can't I suck my thumb?"

"Because the dentist said that it would hurt your teeth."

Claire thought for a moment, then asked, "Can I still pick my nose?"

Mingle a little folly with your wisdom; a little nonsense now and then is pleasant.   CARMEN HORACE

Vice goes a long way tow'rd makin' life bearable. A little vice now and then is relished be th' best of men.
FINLEY PETER DUNN

More Where That Came From

Charles, Age 3

Mr. Jones offered Charles a shiny red apple. Charles grabbed the apple and took a bite.

His father seized the opportunity to teach the boy some manners. "What are you going to say, Charles?"

Without hesitation, Charles looked at Mr. Jones and said, "You got any more?"

An "attitude of gratitude" . . . or "needy and greedy?" Which pattern describes our lives?

Previous generations sang an old hymn that went like this . . .

> *"When you're worried and cannot sleep,*
> *Count your blessings instead of sheep,*
> *And you'll fall asleep*
> *Counting your blessings."*

Return to Sender

Nicki, Age 3

A new baby sister. Wow!

Nicki was so happy when they brought the baby home. Then the new wore off, and routine set in. The crying during the night disturbed the sleep of one and all.

As Nicki was saying her prayers, her mother overheard these words: "Dear Lord, please take Tiffany back to heaven to be with *You* . . . she's driving us *crazy!*"

> *I have lived to thank God that all my prayers have not been answered.*   JEAN INGELOW

Stranger Danger

Randy, Age 5

The first day of kindergarten was over. Randy could hardly wait to tell his mom what he had learned.

As they pulled away from the curb, he said in his most grown-up voice, "Mama . . . you do not have to worry. I will NEVER get in a car with a stranger!"

"That's great, Randy," she said. "I'm very proud of you."

After the slightest hesitation, he spoke again. "Mama," he said, "what's a stranger?"

Check It Out

Greg, Age 4
Son of Beverly Smallwood

As his mom shopped for household essentials, Greg spotted a shiny yellow truck.

"Will you *please* get it for me?" he begged. It was the third toy he had asked for in an hour.

"No, we can't get it, Greg," she responded. "I don't have enough money."

"Yes, you do. I know you have money," he countered. "When you opened your purse, I saw—you still have more *checks!*"

Which Ditch Is Which?

Danny, Age 4

Danny was riding in the family car with his parents. He was aware that his dad hated back seat drivers. Suddenly, out of nowhere, a car was in their lane, coming toward them.

Danny's eyes darted toward his dad as he shouted, "Dad! You are going into the ditch! But," he added, not wanting to be critical, "this is a *good* ditch!"

When you come to a fork in the road, take it.
YOGI BERRA

Picture This

Margaret, Age 9

Margaret skipped into the kitchen, ready for the day ahead. She was wearing a bright T-shirt and gym shorts, not the usual school attire.

Her daddy asked, "What's going on—where are you going?"

Margaret answered with great confidence, "I'm going to field day—to pick up my blue ribbons."

And she did!

After the Green Bay Packers won Super Bowl XXXI, newspapers carried the story that, as a child, Brett Favre had said, "I'm gonna quarterback in the Super Bowl, and I'm gonna win."

And he did!

> *I visualized where I wanted to be, what kind of player I wanted to become. I knew exactly where I wanted to go, and I focused on getting there.*
> MICHAEL JORDAN

> *Dream lofty dreams and as you dream, so shall you become; your vision is the promise of what you shall one day be.* JAMES ALLEN

Where's the Rub?

Molly, Age 2
Daughter of Judy Moon Denson

When it was bath time for Molly, her mother would take a bar of soap and rub it back and forth on the bath cloth to work up a good lather. This time Molly anticipated the ritual.

She handed the soap and the bath cloth to her mother and said, "Here. Wash the soap."

One Man *Stans* Alone

Katie, Age 8

Katie was waiting when her dad came home from work.

"Dad," she said, "who is Richard Stans?"

"Richard Stans? I don't know. Why do you ask?"

"I just thought he might be important," Katie said, "because when we say the pledge of allegiance we say, 'And to the republic for Richard Stans.' "

Bright Idea

Skip, Age 5

Riding in the back seat of his Mother's car, Skip broke out in song, a favorite from preschool:

"God bless America,
Land that I love,
Stand beside her
And guide her,
Through the night
With a light
From a *bulb!*"

Running on Empty

Brock, AGE 5

Brock's aunt was going through a divorce. She was trying to help her nephew understand that his uncle had moved out and that he wouldn't be living with her any more. It was not an easy conversation. The "why's" were hard to avoid and even harder to explain. Time passed as they both sat quietly and reflected on what had been said.

Finally, Brock said thoughtfully, "Well, I guess he just wan out of wove!"

The true course of love never runs smooth.

SHAKESPEARE

We are not the same persons this year as last; nor are those we love. It is a happy chance if we, changing, continue to love a changed person.

W. SOMMERSET MAUGHAM

Senior Class

Anna, Age 5

Anna's parents took her to visit her great-grand-parents. She was intrigued by the fact that Big Paw Paw had lived so many years, as evidenced by the character lines on his face.

"How old *are* you?" she asked.

"I'm 81," he replied.

"Wow! How *high* do you plan to go?"

Our obsession with youth makes us want to ignore and avoid aging. The truth is, nobody we know is getting younger.

While few people at 40 are wishing they were 50 or 60, a healthy respect for seniority is important . . . both for the "senior class" and the "undergrads."

At some point, we have more yesterdays than tomorrows. Our focus should not be on how many days we have already used up, but rather on how well we spend the time that remains.

The higher up you go, the more mistakes you're allowed. Right at the top, if you make enough of them, it's considered to be your style.   FRED ASTAIRE

One can never consent to creep when one feels an impulse to soar.   HELEN KELLER

May you live all the days of your life. JONATHAN SWIFT

Win-Win Situation

Sam, Age 4

Sam and his best friend, Jordan, signed up to play T-ball on opposing teams. No problem. In T-ball, everybody bats and runs the bases . . . no need to even keep score.

When game day came, Sam's mom had to be out of town. As soon as she was sure the game was over, she called home to check on him. The phone was ringing as Sam walked in the door.

"How was your game, Sammy?" she inquired hopefully.

"Good," he said.

"Did Jordan do OK, too?"

"Yeah! And you know what else, Mom? We *both* won!"

*Sam had already learned an important lesson—the value of the **double win**. Wise parents help their children grasp this concept early in life.*

*In athletic contests, of course, the goal is to out-score the competition. But should parents' approval of the child rest on his/her performance, or on the final score? Competition can be great . . . if it's **healthy** competition.*

*Conflict can be helpful . . . if it's handled in a way that respects the opinions and feelings of **all involved**.*

*It's good to win . . . if in the process you also **help others win**.*

Role Reversal

Kayleigh, Age 4

Kayleigh's mother was lying on the couch, recovering from a virus. Kayleigh knew immediately what would make the patient feel better: breakfast in bed.

So she served up her best plastic food, on a tiny plastic plate, and poured imaginary juice in a tiny plastic cup.

"Here, sweetie, drink this," she said as she lifted the cup to her mother's lips.

Touched by her little one's tender care, she managed a smile and said, "Are you going to take care of me like this when I'm an old, old lady?"

"Yes," she said sweetly, "if I still have my toy kitchen."

Wishing Well

Ethan, Age 5

It was Christmas time, and Ethan's mother stumped him with a question. "Have you made out your Christmas list yet?" she asked.

"What's a list?" he wanted to know.

His mother explained, and he caught on fast. In fact, a few days later, his Dad asked, "What's on your list, Ethan?"

"Dad," he said, "you'll get old and I'll grow up before I can tell you everything on my list!"

You Can't Go Home Again

Charles Justin, Age 6

Charles Justin invited his best friend to spend the night. It was a tough decision for a little guy who was afraid of getting homesick.

"You might as well get used to it," Charles Justin advised his would-be house guest, "because when you get married, you won't be able to stay with Mama no more!"

A mother is not a person to lean on, but a person to make leaning unnecessary.   DOROTHY CANFIELD FISHER

Don't Wait Too Late

Sam, Age 4

Sam, his mom and dad, and his grandparents were enjoying the evening out at their favorite restaurant.

Predictably, just as dinner was served, Sam announced: "I have to go to the bathroom!"

"Do you have to go right now, or could you wait a little while?" Dad asked.

"Yes, I guess I could," Sam replied, "but I'll have to wiggle a little."

Skin Deep

Annie, Age 8

Annie's dark face was streaked with tears as she returned from the school playground.

"What on earth is wrong, Annie?" her teacher asked.

"Somebody hit me!" Annie sobbed.

"Who was it?"

"It was a white girl," Annie said.

"Do you know the girl's name, or can you at least describe her?" urged her teacher.

"No, I don't know her name," she said, crying even harder. "And I just don't know what else to tell you. Y'all all look alike."

Prejudice is being down on what we're not up on.
UNKNOWN

When you label, you disable.
UNKNOWN

Plus or Minus

Travis, Age 6

Soon after the beginning of the school year, Travis came home and proclaimed, "I'm the smartest math student in the first grade, Dad!"

A few weeks later, Travis brought home a math paper with a big red mark on top.

"What happened to the smartest math student in the first grade?" his dad inquired.

Travis tucked his head and said, "That was before they told me about take-away!"

Just about the time we think we have life conquered, when we breathe a sigh of relief thinking that we have finally "arrived" . . . a new challenge surfaces.

Remember, when we take a step forward, we may temporarily take two steps back . . . losing both confidence and competence. That's normal. Keep stretching . . . keep growing . . . keep moving ahead . . . it's worth it!

All things are hard before they are easy. UNKNOWN

Somewhere Out There

Alex, Age 4

Alex and his dad were driving home from the airport with the moon roof open. Alex put his seat into a reclining position and gazed into the night sky. After a few minutes, he reflected on the wonders of the universe.

"I think God's above the clouds," he said, "but He's not as far away as the stars."

No Name Calling

Michael, Age 8

The children were lining up to go back inside when Michael suddenly broke away from the group and ran to the teacher.

"Teacher, he called me the E-word," he said, pouting and pointing to a boy in line.

"What's the E-word?" the teacher asked.

"You know . . . E-DIOT!"

By Their Fruits
Ye Shall Know Them

Molly, Age 6
Daughter of Judy Moon Denson

As Molly and her mother were walking one day, they saw a "mama" dog.

Molly turned to her mother and said, "Mom, she has puppies. You know how I know?" Pointing to the evidence, she explained, "She has those milk cartons under there."

Sickening Sound

Mollie, Age 8

The Sunday School teacher inquired, "Any prayer requests, anything you'd like us to pray for?"

Mollie's hand shot up. "Pray that my mom will stop throwing up. She's expecting a baby, and she does it all day long!"

The teacher said, "I'm sure your mother will appreciate your concern."

"Yeah, I'm tired of hearing her go *'BLAAAAAH!'* all the time!"

Caught in the Act

Josh, Age 2

Josh's parents were doing their best to potty train him. The baby-sitter was trying to support their efforts. Noticing that the child's pants were wet, she asked the obvious.

"Josh, did you wet your pants?"

He responded, "No. It wained!"

To be perfectly honest, I sometimes find it very difficult to be perfectly honest.   ASHLEIGH BRILLIANT
Pot-Shots epigrams by Ashleigh Brilliant
of Santa Barbara, CA, appear by special permission

Out of Order

Ruth, Age 5

The year was 1943. A group of children were playing quietly as children sometimes did in those days, "not seen and not heard."

Their mothers were at the kitchen table, peeling apples and commiserating about the men in their lives.

"All they do is hunt," one of the wives moaned.

"Yeah, and we have to stay home and keep on working . . ."

Another one picked up the thread, "Yeah, and chase these kids around and wipe their runny noses . . ."

Yet another spoke up, " . . . and *they're* out in the woods, foot loose and fancy free!"

That went on for a while as they took turns rehearsing their pet peeves. The children heard it all.

Finally, Ruth couldn't take it any more. She stuck her head around the door facing and said, "I'm going to be an old maid . . . and I'm going to tell *all my children* to be old maids, too!

Practice Makes Perfect

Danny, Age 5

Danny and his mom had to drive to the airport for the first time since they moved to their new home in Phoenix. And, it was one of those days! After running late, taking the wrong turn, then having trouble finding the right gate, Danny's mom was totally frazzled.

Danny leaned over and patted his mother's hand gently.

"It's all right," he said. "It'll be easier the next time. The first time's always the hardest."

Success isn't a destination, it's a journey.   JOHN LEE

What You See ... Is What You Get

Nicole, Age 6

It was Saturday night and Nicole was preparing for a solo in the Sunday morning service at church.

"Are you ready?" her mother asked.

"No," she said.

"Would you like to practice your song one more time?"

"Oh, Mom, I *know* my *song*," she said, "I just don't know what I'm going to *wear!*"

A man, in order to establish himself in the world, does everything he can to appear established there.

LA ROUCHE FOUCAULD

For the Lord sees not as man sees; for man looks on the outward appearance, but the Lord looks on the heart.

I Samuel 16:7

Out of This World

Marcus, Age 7

Marcus and his parents were having dinner at the home of friends. The adults in the group overheard this conversation between Marcus and his playmate:

She: "Do you believe in space aliens?"

He: "Of course! Who else would drive the UFO's?"

Part of the Package

Travis, Age 8

Travis, along with his mother and sister, made weekly visits to see his great-grandmother at the local nursing home. Every single time they went, an elderly gentleman asked him the same question.

"Where'd you get that red hair, boy?" he'd say, forgetting he'd asked before.

The first few times, Travis looked away timidly and made no response. Then one day, the little guy apparently reached the end of his patience. The old man asked one more time, "Where'd you get that red hair, boy?"

Travis took a deep breath and said, "*It came with my head!*"

What's in It for Me?

Chelsie, Age 4

It was a few days before Christmas and the anticipation was almost more than Chelsie could stand. She walked into the family room just as her mom finished wrapping a present.

"Here, put this under the tree," her mom said as she handed the bright, shiny box to Chelsie. "It's for you!"

Chelsie started to shake it the moment she had it in her hand.

"Is it a doll? Is it a game? Or the horses I asked for?" she inquired, looking for clues.

Of course, her mom refused to reveal the contents.

The next morning, Chelsie took a new approach. Shaking the box again, she said, "Mom, I know you're not gonna tell me what's in this present, but just tell me if you think it *sounds* like a doll."

Alone at Last

Shobie, Age 4

Shobie proudly beamed as he called to his mom from across the room, "Mommy, look! I made a picture of you on the computer. You have a smile on your face because you had some quiet time!"

How many of us feel guilty when we relax and "do nothing?" Must we constantly be "productive" in order to earn the right to live on the planet?

As a matter of fact, relaxation is doing something. When we relax, we provide our minds and bodies a time to rejuvenate and an opportunity to make sense of emotions pushed aside.

Quiet time allows us, then, to re-enter to our frenetic schedules with renewed energy, creativity, and insight.

How beautiful it is to do nothing, then rest afterward.
SPANISH PROVERB

S-e-p-a-r-a-t-i-o-n Anxiety

Kayla, Age 3
Daughter of Kym Garraway

Kayla was a child who constantly asked questions. One afternoon she seized the moment to quiz her mother about heaven.

"While we are up there, can we glue, paint and ride our bikes?" she asked.

"Yes," her mother said, "but it will probably be a long time before we get there."

"Well," Kayla said, "if I die before you, would you just come up there for a while?"

Heaven is large, and affords space for all modes of love and fortitude. RALPH WALDO EMERSON

A mother must precede separation with preparation. UNKNOWN

Too Cool For School

Dustin, Age 5

Dustin was excited about riding the big yellow bus to kindergarten. That much he knew. The rest, he wasn't quite sure about.

When the first day was finally over, his mother was waiting at the bus stop to find out how he liked school. She didn't have to wait long for the answer.

"Bye. I won't be seeing you again," Dustin said to the bus driver. "I've had enough of *that!*"

Thou Shalt Not Lie

Sarah, Age 1

Sarah was in the tub, splishing and splashing when her dad walked in. Seeing a puddle on the floor, he said soberly, "Sarah . . . did you do that?"

"No," she said.

"Sarah, are you lying to Daddy?"

"No," she persisted.

"Do you know what lying is?" he tested.

"Yes."

"OK . . . explain lying to Daddy."

Raising her "paws" like the king of the jungle, she said, "Lion goes RRROARRR!"

Nose Dive

Jennifer, Age 3

It was early morning, a busy time for everyone in the house. Jennifer was in no mood to follow routine since she had a cold and felt miserable.

When her mother asked why she was whining, she yelled at the top of her lungs, "My nose won't stop *melting!*"

Mind Your Manners

Jeremy, Age 3

Jeremy was "adjusting" the stereo.

"Don't do that," his mom scolded. "You'll mess it up!"

Testing out his independence, he shot back, "Shut up!"

Horrified, his mother fired back, "WHAT DID YOU SAY?"

Quickly correcting himself, he replied, "I meant, 'Shut up, *please.*' "

Oh Lord, let my words be gracious and tender today, for tomorrow I may have to eat them.
UNKNOWN

Song Gone Wrong

Molly, Age 4
Daughter of Judy Moon Denson

Molly was in deep conversation with her friend Kelly on the phone. Her mother, standing nearby, unobserved, overheard Molly as she broke into song . . . .

"Oh my darling, oh my darling, oh my darling FRANKENSTEIN . . . "

Drawn by Molly in her journal at age 4.

Frankenstein? Darling? Not very! Yet . . . human beings are part "darling" and part "Frankenstein."

Someone said that we spend our courtship looking for things we like in the other person, and we spend the marriage looking for what we don't like! In relationships, we can learn to:

- *appreciate each other's strengths;*
- *shore up each other's weaknesses; and*
- *expect the unexpected—"darling!"*

Keep your eyes wide open before marriage, half shut afterwards.   BENJAMIN FRANKLIN

Mom's Home Cooking

Kara, Age 3

Kara and her dad were enjoying a Saturday morning together while her mom went out shopping.

"What do you want for breakfast?" Dad asked.

"I want eggs and toast, like I always have," his daughter answered.

Kara watched from her stool as her dad scrambled the eggs and popped the toast in the oven. When it was done, he put the plate in front of her and announced, "It's ready."

"No, Daddy, it's not ready yet."

Kara grabbed the golden-brown toast off her plate, dragged the stool to the sink, and proceeded to scrape the toast with a knife, even though it wasn't burned *this* time!

Satisfied, she returned the toast to the plate and said, "Now it's ready!"

Inch By Inch, Life's A Cinch

Letisha, Age 4

Letisha's German Shepherd, Sheba, presented the family with six puppies. As Letisha and her mom delivered the last of the litter to his new home, the child asserted, "Next time, we're going to keep all the puppies."

Her mom asked, "How in the world would we be able to feed all those big dogs?"

Letisha responded confidently, "That's easy. One dog at a time!"

Great things are not done by impulse, but by a series of small things brought together.

VINCENT VAN GOGH

Grain by grain—a loaf; stone upon stone—a palace.

GEORGE BERNARD SHAW

Inside Story

David, Age 5

David fell down and scraped his leg. His grandmother encouraged him, "It's OK. Don't cry . . . you're tough."

"No, I'm not, Grandmama," he cried. "I'm *not* tough on the inside. Nobody is!"

So true, David. Inside, we struggle, yet most of us have learned to live behind masks, pretending we have it all together. But there's a catch. When we fake it, we feel isolated.

While we cannot share our deepest thoughts with everyone we meet, we can cultivate two or three friends who will let down their guard and allow us to do the same.

We were not created to go it alone. Barney, the purple dinosaur, says "I love you . . .you love me."

We say . . . let it be!

Macho does not prove mucho.   ZSA ZSA GABOR

In Step

Megan, Age 4

The old stethoscope had found a home in the toy box. The kids enjoyed talking into it, but seldom put it to its intended use.

This day was the exception. Megan came running to her mother with her eyes as big as saucers.

"Mommy!" she cried, "I hear Jesus' footsteps in my heart!"

> *Every child born into the world is a new thought of God, an ever-fresh and radiant possibility.*
>
> KATE DOUGLAS WIGGIN

In The Name Of God

Kevin, Age 4

"I know what God's name is," Kevin told his mom. "His name is Howard."

"Why on earth do you say his name is Howard?" his mother asked.

He said, "Because, in church we always say, 'Our Father Who art in heaven, *Howard* be thy name.'"

Your Nose Knows

Drew, Age 2

Drew enjoyed crossing his eyes, and when his mom turned around, he was caught practicing . . . again!

"Drew, stop that right now!" his mother scolded. "If you keep crossing your eyes, they will stick together."

"No, they won't," he reasoned. "My nose is between them."

Weight A Minute!

Samantha, Age 4

Samantha was quite pleased with herself. She could now say grace at the table all by herself! There was one prayer that she memorized, word-for-word . . . almost!

"God is great
God is good,
Let us thank Him
For our food.
By His hands,
We are all FAT.
Amen."

I got on the scale and it said, "Come back when you are alone."
                                                                    UNKNOWN

The second day of a diet is always easier than the first . . . by the second day, you're off it!
                                                                    UNKNOWN

Not To Be Denied

Alex, Age 3

It was that special time of year when candy is plentiful: Halloween. Alex knew that peanut butter cups were off limits.

"We have to save them for the trick-or-treaters," his mom reminded him.

Unfortunately, Alex was overcome by temptation. His mother spotted the chocolate smears around his mouth the moment she walked in. "Did you eat the peanut butter cups?" she asked calmly.

Caught red-handed, he came up with a quick (if not perfect) defense. "Mommy, it was an accident," he said. "They fell into my mouth."

Where's the Party?

Katelyn, Age 4

Katelyn and her mom were on their way to a birthday party for Katelyn's friend, Jonathan. They found themselves stalled in the five o'clock rush on Atlanta's perimeter Highway 285.

"Wow, Mommy!" Katelyn said, "Are *all* these people going to Jonathan's birthday party?"

Annual Event

Nathan, Age 8

A specialist came to the classroom to conduct academic evaluations. Nathan was the first one in line.

"When is your birthday?" the specialist asked.
"October 16," he answered.
"What year?"
He sighed, then replied, "Every year."

Live your life, and forget your age.   FRANK BERING

When you were born, you cried and the world rejoiced. Live your life in such a manner that, when you die, the world cries and you rejoice.
                                        OLD INDIAN SAYING

Hysterical-ectomy

Mollie, Age 8

The teacher always began the Sunday School class with prayer. It seemed to help the children settle down and get serious. And to encourage participation, she always asked, "Are there any prayer requests?"

Mollie could only think of one thing, something she'd overheard the grownups discussing. She pieced it together as well as she could and said, "Pray for my neighbor. She lost her uterus last week."

Form vs. Function

Molly, Age 7
Daughter of Judy Moon Denson

Molly's mom had clipped all of her fingernails except the last pinkie.

"Don't cut that one!" Molly said. "I need one to scratch with!"

I have a simple philosophy. Fill what's empty. Empty what's full. And scratch where it itches.
ALICE ROOSEVELT LONGWORTH

Eye of the Beholder

ge 6; Jon, Age 7; Kendall, Age 7

entrepreneurial spirit was alive and well. The makeshift "store" beside the road was staffed with three smiling, eager business owners . . . Ashley, Jon, and Kendall.

The bright red paint on the large sign over the stand invited passersby to stop. It said:

The Devil Made Me Do It!

David, Age 3

When David threw his ball, it rolled into the garage. Uh, oh! He'd better go ask Dad if he could go in there. He'd been told in no uncertain terms that the garage . . . more particularly, the new ski boat in the garage . . . was *off limits!*

"Dad, may I go into the garage to find my ball?"

"I guess so, David. But, remember, don't go near the boat."

A few minutes later, Dad realized that David had not returned. When he went to check on him, sure enough, he saw David perched in the driver's seat of the boat, his little hands turning the wheel, the captain of a fantasy voyage.

"David! What are you doing? You know you're not supposed to be in the boat!"

"Well, Dad," David replied, "I prayed to God to help me find my ball, but hell answered!"

No Tears in Heaven

Jill, Age 3
Daughter of Judy Moon Denson

Jill's friend Mary Katherine lived next door. They played together, but only for short periods because Mary Katherine had to "get her rest." She had been born with a hole in her heart, and the prognosis was grave.

The time came far too soon, just as the doctors had predicted it would. Her life on this earth was over at age 3.

Jill struggled to grasp what it all meant. Her mother explained as best she could that her friend wouldn't have to be sick anymore . . . that now she's in heaven.

Jill said, choking back tears, "Her'll miss her mama."

Our children need our caring help when they're dealing with separation and loss. Unfortunately, many try to protect the child by keeping things "normal and pleasant," as if nothing important has happened.

According to Claudia Jewett in her book, Helping Children Cope with Separation and Loss, *this conspiracy of silence deprives the child of the right to confront and resolve grief. She suggests several ways of helping children deal with loss.*

  • *Provide the comforting presence of a parent or adult whom the child trusts and can rely on in a continuing relationship.*

- *Give prompt and accurate information about what has happened.*
- *Allow the child to ask all kinds of questions, to express any feeling, and to talk about the person who is gone.*
- *Encourage the child's participation in family grieving, including funeral rites.*

Helping a child deal with grief is a difficult task. Its reward is witnessing a child's return to psychological well-being and to a focus on the future.

My Mistake

Jeannette, Age 4

It was one of Mom's unbendable rules—Jeannette and her sister, Becky, had to drink their milk each morning. Jeannette protested every morning, to no avail.

Just after admonishing the girls, "Drink all of your milk," their mom had to leave the kitchen for a moment. Seeing her opportunity, Jeannette hurried to the sink and poured her milk down the drain. Unfortunately for her, her mother returned just in time to see the last drop leave the glass.

"Jeannette! What are you doing?" she asked.

"OOPS!" Jeannette said, "I thought I was pouring it in my mouth!"

Seeing is Believing

Amanda, Age 3

Amanda spent a lot of time at the church because she went to preschool there Monday through Friday.

As her mother came to pick her up, she spotted Reverend Gill across the room waving to her.

"Look, Mom," she said pointing to the minister, "it's the church!"

To Amanda, the preacher and the church were synonymous. That puts a monumental expectation on a mortal being . . . to be everything that is pure and holy . . . God's representative on earth!

When you get right down to it, though, each of us is seen as a representative of something. To the customer, the teller is the bank. To the patient, the nurse is the hospital. The receptionist—even when rude, flustered, uncooperative, demanding—is the clinic.

Our attitudes, our behaviors, our habits—visible to our unseen audiences—reflect on the organizations we represent and the beliefs we hold. What messages do our actions send to the watching world?

Whatever For???

Trevor, Age 4

Trevor was splashing in the pool while his grandmother sat by the edge watching. She turned her head momentarily, and when she looked back again, Trevor had been under water and had come up sputtering and wiping his face.

"Trevor, you put your face under!" she said, knowing he *hated* to do that. "Did you do it on purpose?"

"Yeah," he muttered, "*stupid* purpose!"

Good purposes should be the directors of good actions, not the apology for bad.   THOMAS FULLER, M.D.

The secret of success is constancy of purpose.
BENJAMIN DISRAELI

Unexpected Turbulence

Alex, Age 4

Alex was on his first flight. When they hit rough air, he was taken by surprise.

He turned to his dad and said, "We must have run over God's big toe!"

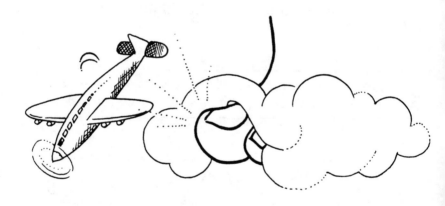

Physically Challenged

Sarah, Age 8

Sarah, who was born with no arms below the elbows and no legs below the knees, had joined her best friend, Tanya, on a family boating excursion. Tanya had managed to wrangle permission from her parents to "drive" the boat.

Eager to be included, Sarah asked, "May I have a turn?" Cautiously, Tanya's parents agreed. Things went well . . . at first. Then, the young driver veered off course. Tanya quickly reached over and grabbed the steering wheel.

Sarah was indignant. "You do it your way, and I'll do it mine," she said. "What do you think I am . . . HANDICAPPED?"

I have learned to deal with a deteriorating body without giving up. Every time something goes, I turn to what's left and figure out a way to use it. I keep my **purpose** *in mind . . . to be a blessing to others. Sometimes people don't understand that, inside, we're just like they are . . . feelings, hopes, ambitions, needs. They assume we are different, and they stay away. I try to understand, refusing to become bitter and turning my energy into educating others. Most important, I keep my faith in God. He's given me so much . . . a good brain, gifts to relate to people, strength to cope with difficulty. I'm thankful!*

PAM WHITE, age 37
Diagnosed with muscular dystrophy at age 11
Confined to a wheelchair since age 25

Knowledge is Power

Molly, Age 4
Daughter of Judy Moon Denson

The clip had come off Molly's barrette. She gave the barrette to her mom, who was trying to fix it when Molly grabbed the barrette and took it to her dad.

He was reading the paper but stopped long enough to take a look at the barrette.

"Throw it away. It's broken," he said as he handed it back.

Molly decided to give her mother another chance, and given time, she fixed it.

Molly thanked her mom. Then, as if to console her dad she said, "Oh, well ... you're tougher anyway."

No wonder I'm all confused—one of my parents was a man, the other was a woman.

ASHLEIGH BRILLIANT
Pot-Shots epigrams by Ashleigh Brilliant
of Santa Barbara, CA appear by special permission

Me, Too! Me, Too!

Mollie, Age 3
Becky, Age 8

Mollie and her Mom were taking her sister Becky to school. Without warning, the button popped off Becky's pants.

Becky sucked in her waistline, and patting her tummy, she said, "My pants are too tight!"

"Becky, you and I are going on a diet!" her mother exclaimed.

Never wanting to be left out, Mollie chimed in, "I want to go! I want to go!"

Danger: Overeating may cause you to live beyond your seams!   UNKNOWN

Same Song, Third Verse

Derrick, Age 11

All the aunts, uncles, and cousins for miles around were having a get-together in a nearby town, an event which occurred fairly often.

Something was different this time, though. Now, Scott and Derrick could travel by themselves. Scott had turned sixteen and had received his long-awaited driver's license. Unfortunately, the boys had never paid attention to the directions when their dad was driving. Thus, the stage was set for adventure.

The parents arrived on time, bragging that the boys were "right behind them." An hour passed. No Scott and Derrick.

They began to worry, realizing the boys must be lost.

At last, they arrived, Scott slightly embarrassed, Derrick somewhat perturbed.

"I told Scott, 'I *know* this isn't the right way. We've passed that same dead dog three times!'"

Rained Out

Jane, Age 3

Jane could hear the rain on the roof when she woke up, and that meant no playing outside. She stood by the window, looking with longing at the soggy sod as raindrops splattered on the window sill.

Later in the morning, the sun came out, and her spirits lifted.

"Look, Mom," she said, "I can go outside. God turned the faucet off!"

> *The way I see it, if you want a rainbow, you gotta put up with the rain.* DOLLY PARTON

No Bull!

David, Age 6
Robin, Age 3

Her curiosity got the best of her. Little Robin crawled through the fence to get a closer look at the calf in the pen behind their country home.

The calf was not amused! He lowered his head and ran toward the little girl, who was now escaping through that fence in record time, screaming all the way!

Her brother David witnessed the entire incident. He tried to comfort his scared little sister and warn her at the same time.

"Why did you go in that pen with that calf, Robin? Don't you know that his daddy *could* have been a *bull?*"

The secret of success is not to make the wrong mistakes.
YOGI BERRA

If I Had A Hammer

Amy, Age 3

Amy "whopped" her 18-month-old sister, Margaret, on the head with a toy hammer.
"Amy, why did you do that?" her daddy scolded.
"Well, Daddy," she reasoned, "sometimes the good just runs out!"

Patience is a virtue . . . unless it's taken to the extreme. Doormats get no respect.

Maybe you've tried to "keep the peace" in a relationship by "taking and taking." (Is that real peace?)

*We're not recommending a hammer. We **are** recommending balance . . . your rights **and** the other person's rights.*

When there is reciprocity and mutual respect, the good won't run out!

Five and Holding

Ward, Age 5

All his life Ward had looked forward to the next birthday with a twinkle in his eye. But not this one. His grandmother was the first to pick up on it.

"Why aren't you excited about your birthday, Ward?"

"Because," he said, looking worried, "when you're six, you have to read, and I don't know how."

New experiences. New stages of life. New opportunities. Meeting life head-on is not easy. We tend to play a game of "what if?" We fear the unknowns that lie ahead. To complicate matters, we discount our capabilities.

Perhaps we should adopt the philosophy of Dr. Susan Jeffers, who admonishes us to "feel the fear, and do it anyway"! Instead of asking, "What if?", imagine what can happen if we ask, "What's next?"

Faith came singing into my room,
And other guests took flight.
Grief, anxiety, fear and gloom,
Sped out into the night.

ELIZABETH CHENEY

Tight Squeeze

Shacha, Age 5

Shacha's baby-sitter, Elaine, was casually flipping through the pages of a fashion magazine, stopping now and then to study the attire being presented.

Shacha was looking on with interest. "She's sexy," he said, seeing a scantily-clad model.

Surprised at the remark, Elaine said, "What's *sexy?*"

He shot right back. "Beautiful ladies with clothes that are too small for them."

Mind Over Matter

Nikki, Age 3

Nikki sat at the kitchen table, staring thoughtfully at the wall. She rose from her chair, walked to the wall, touched it with her nose, then returned to her chair.

She sat quietly for a few minutes, then went to the wall again, this time laying her right palm against the flat surface. By now she had attracted her mother's attention. Mom observed in silence as Nikki returned to her "thinking chair." Now for the third time she walked to the wall and leaned her entire body into it for a few seconds.

Suddenly, Nikki began dancing around the room, clapping her little hands.

"What's happening, Nikki?" her mother asked.

"I figured it out!" she answered, still bouncing. "It's my brain that tells my body what to do!"

Psychologists today have discovered what King Solomon knew thousands of years ago: "As a man thinks in his heart, so is he."

Our thoughts give birth to our feelings, our motives, our actions, our habits . . . literally, to our destinies.

Positive vs. negative, optimistic vs. pessimistic, encouraging vs. critical, courageous vs. fearful . . . which thoughts do we allow to control our minds? We have the power to choose.

Who Dunnit?

Robert, Age 5

Robert had been "into everything" that day at his grandmother's house. When a vase turned up broken, his grandmother said, "Did you do that, Robert?" She knew full well he had ... *that* and *more!*

After several incidents, she called his name *again.* "ROBERT ... "

His "defense" was all encompassing, if not airtight.

"Whatever I did," he said, "I didn't do it!"

To deny all is to confess all.   SPANISH PROVERB

Gone Astray

Jesse, Age 5

Goldie, the family dog, was just days away from delivering puppies. She led a charmed life in the country, and she had the run of the place. There were times when no one knew her exact whereabouts.

And so it was that a certain air of mystery surrounded the coming event. When someone asked Jesse what he thought the little dogs would look like, he explained that no one knew.

He said simply, "We're not sure who she married!"

Good Question!

Katie, Age 5

Soon after Katie's Aunt Pat had died of cancer, the child's beloved pet died. Her parents explained to her that Charlie had gone to heaven to be with Aunt Pat.

Without missing a beat, Katie replied, "Why would Aunt Pat want a dead dog?"

Flattery Will Get You Nowhere

Beth Ann, Age 5

Beth Ann had her eye on one particular toy at K-Mart, something she had wanted for quite a while. She asked her mom if they could go there and buy it.

"Not today," her mom said.

All was quiet for a moment as Beth Ann contemplated a strategy that could get her mom into the store.

"Mom," she said in her most cunning voice, "you know ... you look soooooo thin when you're pushing the cart at K-Mart!"

Fly By Night

Krystal, Age 8

"All the kids at school have been arguing about whether there really is a Santa Claus," Krystal told her friend.

"What do you think?" her friend asked.

"Well, I believe in Santa Claus," Krystal replied. Then lowering her voice, she added, "But I'm just not sure about those flying reindeer!"

Please don't spoil everything by telling me the truth.

ASHLEIGH BRILLIANT
Pot-Shots epigrams by Ashleigh Brilliant
of Santa Barbara, CA, appear by special permission

---

*The truth **can** hurt. We often experience pain and disappointment, short term. In the long run? Knowing the truth helps us identify the real issues and resolve them.*

You will know the truth, and the truth will set you free. JESUS CHRIST, *John 8:32*

Fill in the Blanks

Molly, Age 5
Daughter of Judy Moon Denson

During his Sunday morning sermon, the preacher walked away from the pulpit and stood directly in front of the congregation. As was their custom, the Densons were sitting in the very first pew.

Arms waving, robes flowing, Reverend Smith loudly proclaimed the truth. With extra emphasis, he posed the rhetorical question: *"Do you believe it?"*

There was a pregnant pause ... then Molly's voice rang out, **"Or not!"**

Molly's question is echoed in the hearts of children everywhere: "Mom and Dad, do you really 'believe it' ... or not?"

How do they know? They watch! Our values show in the way we live.

You tell them it's wrong to steal ... but when the clerk gives you too much change, you simply say, "This is my lucky day!" and put it in your pocket.

You tell them it's wrong to lie ... then the phone rings, it's for you, and you say, "Tell him I'm not home."

Seeing is believing. When our children see us in action, do they believe we "believe it ... or not?"

What you are shouts louder than what you say.
                                             UNKNOWN

To "Be" or Not To "Be"

Toby, Age 3
Grandson of Glenna Salsbury, CSP, CPAE
Professional Speaker, Trainer, Consultant
Author, *The Art of the Fresh Start*

During a casual afternoon conversation, Toby's mom asked him, "What does Grandma GiGi do?"

"She works with paper," the little fellow answered, having seen her working on her book when he visited.

His other grandmother was a museum guide. His mother quizzed him further, "So, Toby, what does Grandma Barbara do?"

"She walks around a lot," Toby replied matter-of-factly.

Fascinated with his perceptions, his mom couldn't resist asking, "Well, what do *I* do?"

Without hesitation, Toby responded, "You make lists."

Life . . . seen through the eyes of a child.

It's easy to mistake urgency for importance. Which is better: to check one more thing off the to-do list; or to slow down and spend time alone (or with special people) . . . reflecting, planning, relaxing, or just "being"?

Our God-given value is not contingent on our staying in a full-speed-ahead performance mode. Discovering this, we can give ourselves permission to **be** *. . . in essence, a "human being" rather than a "human doing."*

Good Heavens

Danny, Age 3

Danny and his dad went for a ride on a gorgeous, blue-sky day. After a while, clouds began to appear on the horizon. Then more clouds moved in.

From his car seat, Danny observed, "Dad, the clouds are eating up the sky!"

"HI" in the Sky

Kathryn, Age 3

Kathryn was clear about one of nature's mysteries. She summed it up this way:

"Fog is just clouds coming down to say 'Hi!' "

Big Foot

Mandy, Age 5

The family was driving home from a new church they had visited. They were discussing the positives and the negatives about joining it.

Mandy spoke up.

"I don't want to go back to that church."

"Why?" her dad asked.

"Didn't you hear what that preacher said?"

"What?" her dad asked.

"He said he didn't care whose toes he stepped on—and did you see how *big* he was?"

How Bad Can It Be?

Molly, Age 7
Daughter of Judy Moon Denson

It was summertime, and Molly loved to spend time with her live-in grandmother, Mamaw Moon. Mamaw had developed a strong attachment to the afternoon soap opera, "Days of Our Lives." Predictably, in no time, Molly was hooked, too.

One day, Molly's mother happened to come home early from work. Concerned, she scolded, "Molly, this has to stop! I will not allow you to watch that show any more."

"Why not?" Molly protested. "They hardly ever kill anybody. And if they do . . . they come back!"

It's a popular plot on the soaps. A plane goes down and is lost . . . no bodies are found . . . then it happens. They bring the character back, still alive, but with amnesia.

In TV drama, they can "write you back in." But where are those writers when ***you*** *need a new story line in* ***your*** *life?*

Sometimes it is easier to create illusions than to find real happiness. "I'll be happy . . . when we live in a bigger house . . . when my husband spends more time with me . . . when I lose 20 pounds."

Create a realistic *strategy to begin again.* The Art of the Fresh Start, *by Glenna Salsbury is a great resource for your planning.*

A good beginning makes a good ending.

ENGLISH PROVERB

Fielder's Choice

Amy, Age 9
Daughter of Beverly Smallwood

Amy was still getting used to the idea that her newly-single mom was starting to date.

"Let's talk, girl to girl," Amy said one night as her mother came in. "Tell me all about your evening."

"Well, I guess it was OK, but, to tell you the truth, he was kind of a nerd."

"A nerd! What are you doing . . . going out with nerds?"

"Well, Amy, it's somewhere to go, someone to go out with."

"Mom! It's just like the coach told us in baseball. *You don't have to swing at every one they throw you!*"

Life has a way of throwing us curve balls. Things don't always happen the way we plan and dream. However, we can **choose** *how to respond. We can:*

- *focus on those things which* **can** *be controlled;*
- *work on our* **own** *habits that contributed to the problem;*
- *stay out of the trap of bitterness;*
- *refuse to become helpless, blaming, or irresponsible;*
- *use painful experiences to empathize with others;*
- *determine to bring good out of a bad situation by* **learning** *from it!*

> *When one man was asked how he was doing, he whined, "I'm doing fairly well, under the circumstances."*
>
> *His optimistic friend replied, "What are you doing **under** the circumstances?* UNKNOWN

A Question of Suitability

Kirby, Age 10

When Mom went in to read the kids to sleep, she found them watching a TV drama, "The Pretender."

"This doesn't look like a very good show to be watching," she commented.

"But there hasn't been a single gunshot," Kirby protested, "and it didn't say 'parental excretion devised'!"

Low Blow

John Logan, Age 6
Nathanael, Age 5

A familiar line from the popular Christmas carol, "Away in a Manger," goes like this: *"The cattle are lowing, the baby awakes..."*

John Logan and Nathanael had their own version, and sang it with gusto.

"The cattle are blowing the baby away..."

Here, There, and Everywhere

Megan, Age 7

Megan's grandmother was reading aloud the story of Johnny Appleseed. Megan listened intently to the part about how Johnny planted seeds everywhere he went!

When the story ended, her grandmother said, "Well, Megan what did you learn?"

Megan responded tentatively, "That he was a trespasser?"

Even if I knew tomorrow the world would go to pieces, I would still plant my apple tree. MARTIN LUTHER

Hitting Below the Belt

John, Age 7

John, who had spent Saturday night with a friend, telephoned his mother on Sunday morning.

"They've invited me to go fishing today. May I go?"

"No, son. Today is Sunday, the day we go to church. Maybe you can go another time."

Irritated, John hung up the phone and went home.

He appeared at his mother's bedroom door just as she struggled with a tight girdle, determined to pull it up.

"Why are you doing that?" John smirked. "Everyone in church *knows* you're too fat!"

It is folly to punish your neighbor by fire when you live next door. PUBLILUS SYRUS

How Much is Enough?

Kayla, Age 3
Daughter of Kym Garraway

It was Grandparents' Day at Kayla's preschool. All four of her grandparents were there, along with Kayla's mom.

Kayla asked, "Aren't daddies allowed to come?" Her mother answered, "Yes, but Daddy has to work to make us a living . . . to give us food and clothing and, you know, to make money."

Having seen five dollars in her mother's purse earlier that morning, Kayla said, "But we HAVE money!"

Drawing by Kayla Garraway.

Not what we have, but what we enjoy, constitutes our abundance.   I. PETIT SINN

Credit cards are okay for some people, but I wouldn't go for one. I try not to spend money that I don't have buying what I can't afford.   OSEOLA MCCARTY
Author, *Simple Wisdom for Rich Living*

Time is Money

Brennan, Age 3

Brennan was sad as his mom left for work. His mom and dad had explained, "With Dad in school, Mom is the breadwinner of the family. She goes to work because that's where the money comes from to buy things we need."

The next week, Mom took Brennan to the office for a little while, thinking it might make things easier for him, knowing where she spent her days.

He just had one question after looking around. *"Where's the money?"*

Thirty-Six Long

Trey, Age 4

Trey and his mom had moved in with 'Me-ma,' his grandmother.

One morning, his mom stepped out of the shower just as he walked into the room. He stood and stared for a moment.

Pointing at her chest, he observed, "Me-ma's are *longer!*"

Crime and Punishment

Megan, Age 3

Megan was very good at dreaming up ways to put off going to sleep. One night, she had exhausted her list of delays . . . water, the bathroom, more water, monsters under the bed, one more story.

Finally, her mother warned, "Megan, I don't want to hear one more peep out of you tonight, not another sound, or you're going to get a spanking. Do you understand?"

Megan nodded.

"Now go to sleep," her mother said firmly, then left the room.

All was quiet on the home front, but not for long. "Maa-maa!" Megan called out cheerfully, "Come on in here and 'pank me, 'cause I want some JUICE!"

Megan had already learned what many adults have not. Choices have consequences.

Here are some timely questions to answer about taking risks before you act:

1. *What's the worst that could happen?*
2. *If the worst did happen, how would I handle it?*
3. *Are the benefits I expect so valuable to me that they are worth the risk I will be taking?*

Think about it . . . sleep on it several nights . . . and proceed, only if the light is bright green!

Hold That Thought

Eli, Age 5

Eli's mom poured some Coke into a glass "for the road." As she backed out of the driveway and started down the street, she took a sip.

Remembering a lecture from school, Eli said sternly: "Mama, mama! Don't you know you're not supposed to drink and drive?"

The driver is safer when the roads are dry. The roads are safer when the driver is dry.　　UNKNOWN

The hand that lifts the cup that cheers, should not be used to shift the gears.　　UNKNOWN

Gimme Five!

Matthew, Age 5

Shortly after Matthew's birthday, a family friend asked, "How old are you, Matthew?"

Holding up five fingers, he answered proudly, "I'm a whole hand!"

Drawing by Mercer Ann McKee

Going My Way?

Marcie, Age 2
Daughter of Connie Podesta, M.S.
Co-Author, *How to Be the Person Successful Companies Fight to Keep*
Comedienne, International Speaker

Marcie was in one of those moods that two-year-olds are known for: TERRIBLE! When she wouldn't stop whining, her mother finally said, "Marcie, that's enough. Go to your room."

"Fine," she said through pouted lips with hands on hips. "I was going there anyway!"

Hook, Line, and Stinker

Chelsea, Age 6

Chelsea was very excited about her first fishing trip with her friend, Alex. Things were going nicely, when suddenly Chelsea screamed, "Help, help! Something's wrong!"

Alex's dad, Eric, looked to find Chelsea leaning backward, struggling with the pole. Obviously, she had a fish on the line. "Reel it in, Chelsea, reel it in!" he said.

"No way!" she answered. "You do it!"

Eric landed it and held the fish up for Chelsea to see. She grimaced at the prickly fins and the fishy smell and said, "Well! If *that's* gonna happen, I'm not doing this any more. Let's go home!"

Like Chelsea, we sometimes take on projects, expecting them to be "fun," not fully realizing that there will be "struggles and stinky parts." Nowhere is this more evident than when we work with little people in helping roles such as mother, father, grandparent, or with big people as supervisor, coach, counselor, or friend.

When disappointments come, do you become disgusted, give up and "go home"?

Never give up, for that is just the place and time that the tide will turn.   HARRIET BEECHER STOWE

Success seems to be largely a matter of hanging on after others have let go.   WILLIAM FEATHER

Consider the Source

Carson, Age 5

When Carson's older brother lost a tooth, Carson asked if he could have it. His mother chimed in, "What are you going to do with it?"

"Put it under my pillow and get the money," he said.

"If the tooth fairy finds out you tricked her, she won't be too happy," she warned.

"How would she know?" he asked.

"Your teeth are smaller, and you don't have an empty spot in your mouth."

He looked at his mom, the truth suddenly dawning on him, and he said, "There's no such thing as the tooth fairy."

"Who do you think gives the money?" she asked.

He answered with a grin, "Santa!"

For Everything, There is A Season

Greg , Age 6
Son of Beverly Smallwood

"I want my horse to have a baby colt so I'll have two horses to ride," Greg told his dad.

"She can't have a colt right now," explained his dad. "We'll have to wait until she's in heat."

Later that summer day, Greg yelled for his dad and mom to come outside. What a sight! The horse was soaked in perspiration, panting for breath. Sweat rolled down Greg's chubby, beet-red cheeks.

"We're gonna get our colt," he said. "I've ridden her around and around the house, and now she's in heat!"

A watched pot never boils.   UNKNOWN

Timing is everything.   UNKNOWN

It's Written All Over Your Face

Brittany, Age 4

As Brittany and her aunt pulled up to the drive-in window of the bank, her aunt said, "If you're sweet, the lady at the window will give you a piece of candy."

"I am sweet," Brittany said.

"How does the lady know that?" her aunt teased.

With a big smile, Brittany said, "Just look at this face!"

Of all the things you wear, your expression is the most important.   UNKNOWN

Facts of Life

Jonathan, Age 4

It was late at night when Jonathan's mother felt the first labor pains. In fact, Jonathan was sound asleep when his dad picked him up out of his bed and dropped him off at his grandparents' house.

When he woke up the next morning, his grandmother shared the exciting news: "You have a new baby sister, Jonathan!"

"Oh, boy," he squealed, "Does my mama know it?"

(Does she ever!)

Gone, But Not Forgotten

Nancy, Age 4

Nancy's church offered a special service just for children known as "Children's Church."

"Any prayer requests today?" the leader asked the children.

"Pray for my grandmother," Nancy said in a serious tone of voice.

"Is she sick?" the leader asked.

"No, she's dead. She died about three years ago."

Early Economics

Christy, Age 7

It was Christy's first away-from-home camp. Soon after her arrival, Christy's friends taught her how to get the operator on the pay phone and call collect. Her parents were glad to hear from her . . . the first night . . . and again the next morning . . . and again after lunch.

But when the phone rang again after dinner, something had to be said. "Are you homesick?" her mom inquired.

"No, I'm not homesick. I just wanted to chat."

"Christy," Mom said, "We love to hear from you, but you can't call home three times a day. It's expensive!"

Christy answered, "No it's not, Mama. It doesn't cost anything. I get my quarter back every time!"

Nowadays, a dollar saved is a quarter earned.
BOB PHILLIPS

The safest way to double your money is to fold it over once and put it in your pocket. KIN HUBBARD

Gone For Good

Molly, Age 11
Daughter of Judy Moon Denson

In the early nineties, stories about oil spills filled the evening news on a regular basis. Some 20 million gallons leaked out in 1990 alone!

That same year, Molly's class had been studying about renewable resources.

The teacher, wanting to stimulate their thinking, asked, "Is oil a renewable resource, or will it ever run out?"

Molly volunteered, "If we keep spilling it, it will!

Willful waste brings woeful want.   BOB PHILLIPS

How Do I Love Thee?

Jill, Age 9
Daughter of Judy Moon Denson

It was a cold December morning in 1982. The Denson family was eating breakfast and watching "Today" on NBC. Top news topic: the first artificial heart implant. The reporter was explaining the surgical procedure in detail as the camera zoomed in for a close-up.

Jill looked at the mechanical apparatus made of plastic and asked softly, "Can he love people with that heart?"

A merry heart doeth good like a medicine.
KING SOLOMON, Proverbs 17:22

Treasure the love you receive above all. It will survive long after your gold and good health have vanished. OG MANDINO

Long Division

Leigh Anne, Age 7

Leigh Anne's mom and dad were getting a divorce. There was no more putting it off: it was time to tell the children. As their parents talked, the two little girls struggled to make sense of the dreadful news.

Leigh Anne sighed softly. Then with the slightest breath giving sound to her words, she uttered, "This is harder than math!"

Children . . . challenged to stand in a house divided. It's a sad reality that parents often cannot or will not work out their personal differences constructively. It is even sadder when kids are used as pawns in an ongoing battle to "win." When that happens, who wins? NOBODY!

Wise parents care enough to focus on what's best for the children, *not on what's personally beneficial. With mature and cooperative parents (even parents who no longer live together), kids can adjust and ultimately excel—even when life doesn't "add up."*

Two-Fisted Time Line

Whitney, Age 9

Like most children, Whitney couldn't wait for her next birthday. In her mind, this one would be "twice" as significant as the others had been.

"Mom," she said, "when I turn ten, I'll be a double digit!"

Cerebral Suction

Meghi, Age 4

The family drove over a big hill. On the way down, Meghi said, "There's something in my brain and I can't suck it down!"

She was OK after her ears popped.

Color Blind

Chas, Age 5
John, Age 5

Chas, an African-American child, and his Caucasian friend, John, were on the playground. Chas saw his teenage brother across the way with one of *his* Caucasian friends.

"That's my brother!" Chas declared proudly.

"Which one?" John asked, spotting the two boys on the sidewalk.

Chas answered, "The one with the red sweater."

Every bigot was once a child free of prejudice.
SISTER MARY DE LOURDES

Downsizing

Garion, Age 3

Garion's parents took him along to a restaurant that catered to families. Sitting in the next booth was a couple with a newborn baby.

Everyone was oohing and ahhing, the way adults do when they see a baby: "What a doll!"

Garion turned to his folks and said, "When I grow down, *I* want to be a baby."

Eat Those Words

Shannon, Age 4

When Shannon's grandparents came for visits, her "grammy" enjoyed taking the whole family out to dinner. As they packed into the minivan, the subject naturally turned toward where they should dine. Shannon's mom suggested a modestly-priced Mexican place.

"But, Mommy," Shannon said, "I thought you said that when Grammy's here, we can go to all the expensive restaurants!"

So Close and Yet So Far

Lance, Age 5

It was Lance's first T-ball game. He swung—
WHACK!

Lance started to run . . . first base . . . second
base . . . the crowd went wild! As he rounded
third, he could hear their words loud and clear,
"Go home, Lance! Go home!"

Instead of heading for home plate, the little
guy held up, his steps faltering, his heart aching,
his lips quivering. Then came the final blow—
they tagged him out.

He headed toward the gate with their words
still ringing in his ears. With all the courage he
could muster, he turned and yelled back to the
crowd, "OK, then, I WILL go home!"

---

*Many of life's failures are people who did not real-
ize how close they were to success when they gave
up.* THOMAS EDISON

---

*I know you believe you understand what you think
I said, but I am not sure you realize that what you
heard is not what I meant.* UNKNOWN

Lick the Platter Clean

Molly, Age 2
Daughter of Judy Moon Denson

"It's time to feed the kitties, Molly," her mother said.

"*I* want to feed them," she said, reaching for the bowl of leftovers.

Her mother followed her, picking up a spoon to scrape out the dish as they walked out the back door.

Molly looked at her mom, then looked at the cats, and said with authority, "They don't need a spoon!"

Estranged Bedfellows

Cody, Age 5

Cody woke up proud of himself. He had slept all night in his own bed! It had become quite a habit to slip into his mom's bed while his dad was away on business.

"It's time to go to the airport and pick up your dad, Cody," his mother said. "I can't wait to tell him what a big boy you were, sleeping all by yourself."

As they entered the crowded gate area, Cody ran to his dad and announced loudly and proudly, "Guess what, Dad? NOBODY SLEPT WITH MOMMY WHILE YOU WERE GONE!"

Easy Way In

Ian, Age 4

Ian and members of his preschool class were carpooling to the children's symphony. As they approached their destination, the mom who was driving searched for the entrance. She mused aloud, "I wonder where we should go in?" Ian responded, "A door is always a good choice!"

When one door closes, another opens; but we often look so long and so regretfully upon the closed door that we do not see the one which has opened for us.

ALEXANDER GRAHAM BELL

If you don't hear opportunity knocking, find another door.

UNKNOWN

Smile and the World Smiles With You

Paul, Age 4

It was a crystal clear night. A myriad of stars made the perfect backdrop for a fingernail moon, turned up at the corners.

Paul spotted it from the bedroom window and said, "Look, Mom. The world is smiling!"

When Paul looked out at the world, he saw it smiling at him. How wonderful it is that he is already learning to be optimistic! Many years of research by Dr. Martin Seligman (The Optimistic Child), *have demonstrated that the optimistic child is safeguarded against depression and experiences unusual resilience throughout life.*

Parents can help children develop habits of optimism in several ways:

- *Become a model of optimism.*
- *Give kids realistic challenges that lead to successful mastery in a variety of areas.*
- *Emphasize the kid's own "smart parts."*
- *Lovingly teach the child to develop optimism by challenging negative thought habits.*

Like Father, Like Son

Zachary, Age 4

Zachary was not fond of taking a nap, so his dad agreed to lie down beside him to make it more appealing to the little guy. Zachary, however, recognized the opportunity to "relate."

"Daddy, we both have brown hair," he said as he stroked his dad's hair.

"Yes, we do," his dad said simply, taking the conversation no further and closing his eyes to encourage the same from Zachary.

Zachary reached over and touched his dad's eyelids and said, "And we both have black eyes."

"Yes," his dad said, giving the shortest answer possible.

But Zachary would have the last word. He touched his dad's ear and said, "And—I'm *trying* to grow me some big ears."

Do's and Don't's

Hans, Age 7

After a bedtime story, Hans' mother asked him what he knew about the Ten Commandments.

Hans replied, "I don't know all of them, but I know the most important one."

"Which one is that?" she asked.

Hans said, "Keep your hands, feet and other objects to yourself."

Come to think of it, Hans, keeping a commandment like that would solve many problems!

When Jesus was asked about the "greatest" commandment, He summed up all the laws with one word, "Love".

"Love God with all your heart, and love your neighbor as yourself."

Notice that "LOVE" is a verb, an action word. The truth is, when we are acting out of love for God and others, we don't steal, kill, or talk about our neighbor.

The "don't's" fade into the background when we concentrate on the "do's" of living in love.

Sub Zero

Kristin, Age 5

Kristin was playing with her friend, Jason, who was two years old. They heard a knock on the door.

It was a family friend and her two-month-old baby. Jason wanted the baby to come play with them, too.

Kristin, older and wiser, explained that the baby was too young to play. After several attempts to get through to him, she finally came up with an example he could understand.

"You know, Jason, how I'm five and you're two? Well, this baby is so little it doesn't even have a number yet!"

Such is Life!

Danny, Age 8

The adjustment to being back in school after summer vacation was far from over. Every morning, Danny's mom found it to be a challenge to get him out from under the covers. That dreaded morning chore behind her one more time, she went downstairs to start breakfast.

A few minutes later, she glanced at the top of the stairs. There sat Danny, hair standing straight up, his big white T-shirt pulled down over his knees, his hands propping up his chin. He was talking to no one in particular.

"I get up in the morning," he mumbled. "I eat breakfast. I go to school. I come home. I eat a snack. I go to tennis lessons. I practice my piano. I do my homework. I eat my dinner. I read a book. I go to bed. *Is this all there is to life?*"

What lies behind us and what lies before us are small matters compared to what lies within us.

RALPH WALDO EMERSON

So Be It

Amy, Age 5

Amy's parents were teaching her to say grace before each meal. One day Amy said the blessing:

> *"God is great, God is good,*
> *Let us thank Him for our food.*
> *By His hands we all are fed.*
> *Give us, Lord, our daily bread.*
> *I mean it!"*

As Amy opened her eyes, her mother heaped on the praise. "Amy, that was just great! You remembered the whole thing and said it so well." Then she added gently, "But I didn't quite understand why you said, 'I mean it!' at the end of your prayer."

Amy answered, "Well, Mama, that's what the preacher always says at the end of his prayers!"

She's All Yours!

Josh, Age 2

Josh's "Pa Paw" had a habit of teasing him when he dropped by to visit. He would walk over and give Trudy, his daughter, and Josh's mom, a hug.

"*My* Trudy," he'd say, without taking his eyes off Josh.

Josh would say, "No, *my Trudy!*"

The game always went the same . . . that is, until the day that Josh's mom had scolded him just before his granddad walked in.

Without noticing Josh's sour expression, Pa Paw began the ritual. "*My* Trudy," he said, right on schedule.

Josh blurted out, "HAVE her!"

Like Pulling Teeth

Molly, Age 2
Daughter of Judy Moon Denson

Molly's grandmother wore dentures. Each night, she would remove them for a thorough cleaning. Molly observed the procedure and tugged on her own teeth in like manner.

She looked up at her grandmother and said, "Mine are stuck."

Bruised Ego

Amos, Age 4

"I had a dweam last night," Amos told his mother. "I dweamed I was in my bwue monster twuck on the woad, and I fell out!"

"Did you get hurt?" she asked.

"Nope," he said, "just my feelings."

> *A mother's sympathy serves as an emotional Band-Aid for a bruised ego.*   HAIM G. GINOTT

The Great Outdoors

Teresa, Age 5

The kindergarten teacher posed a question to the class: "Who can name the four seasons?" No one knew the answer at first. Then Teresa waved her hand in the air.

"What are they?" the teacher prompted.

She answered confidently, "Deer season, quail season, squirrel season, and duck season."

Don't Take No For An Answer

Ryan, Age 5

Ryan begged his Mom, "Mommy, can I have just ONE piece of candy?"

"No," she said firmly.

Undaunted, Ryan persisted. "Well, then, how many pieces *can* I have?"

The optimist proclaims that we live in the best of all possible worlds; and the pessimist fears this is true.

JAMES BRANCH

All that is necessary to break the spell of inertia and frustration is this: Act as if it were impossible to fail.

DOROTHY BRANDE

The Big Picture

Ebony, Age 11

Joshua, Age 6

"I want to go up into outer space," Ebony said.

"Why?" his mom asked.

"To see how pretty it looks," he said.

Joshua had a better idea.

"Wait 'til you get to heaven," he said. "You'll have a better view from there."

Silent Suffering

William and Matthew, Age 9

The twins' parents had been married for years when the boys appeared on the scene. From the day William and Matthew were born, they were showered with affection.

Then, one day, their world came crashing down: their mother was diagnosed with cancer. An extended stay in the hospital was inevitable, the prognosis bleak.

During the long months that followed, the boys stayed with their grandmother and with other relatives and friends. Every effort was made to make their lives as normal as possible, and on the surface, it was. They preferred to keep their feelings about their mother's condition to themselves.

On Father's Day, their dad left their mother's side to spend the day with them. As the family sat down to eat, William asked if he could say the blessing. With every head bowed, he was able to express his feelings openly for the first time.

"Dear Father, bless Mama and Daddy and help Mama to get well. Bless our aunts and uncles and all our friends who have taken care of us. And especially bless grandmother ... she has suffered the most because Mama is her daughter. Amen."

*Suffering in silence. We want to believe that if we don't say it "out loud," nobody will **feel** it. Children need a chance to voice their feelings. The adults around them can help them do that. How?*
Watch for signals they give, such as:
   • *acting out or misbehaving;*
   • *withdrawing from family members;*
   • *cutting off contact with friends.*
Draw them out with words like these:
   • *"Tell me more."*
   • *"If I were your age, I might feel the same way."*
   • *"Why do you ask?"*
   • *"What bothers you the most?"*
   • *"How can I help?"*

The Only Lonely

Krystal, Age 9

Krystal was outgoing and articulate... "normally." But not anymore. Her parents' divorce was official now.

Her mom found a house in the same town, but in a new school district. They moved in just in time for the fall semester. The first few days in school were especially difficult. Then Krystal became acquainted with some of her new classmates.

"I'm feeling a little better now," she confided to her mom. "At first I thought *I* was the only kid who was divorced."

Kids do carry our pain. In Krystal's case, she felt as though she herself was divorced.

*Divorce may be the only answer in some situations. But even then, it's never an **easy** answer, especially when children are involved.*

If parents can set aside egos and hurts, they can give children permission to love and have a relationship with each parent . . . without apology.

You will find as you look back upon your life, that the moments when you have really lived, are the moments when you have done things in the spirit of love. HENRY DRUMMOND

Too Much of a Good Thing

Julie, Age 3

Christmas... 'tis the season to be jolly. However, all that merriment takes its toll on energy and endurance. That was the case with Julie and her mom.

The two of them had spent the entire morning in a very crowded mall. Even though the day had been especially tiring, they proceeded to bake cookies when they got home. Why? Because that was the *plan!* Her mom had said they would bake cookies *today*, and that's just what they would do!

Christmas cheer, however, was not to be found in the measuring, mixing and molding. In fact, Julie's mom was grumbling under her breath all the while, her good intentions overcome by exhaustion.

Finally, Julie let out a long sigh and said, "Mommy, are we almost done making memories?"

Missing Person(s)

Lauren, Age 10

Lauren was visiting her aunt's ranch in Idaho for the summer. A month went by before she bothered to write to the folks back home ... her parents, her brother, and her sister. The postcard read:

"I miss *some* of you.

Having a great time."

Lauren

That's A No-No

Mary Margaret, Age 3

Mary Margaret ran to her mother, obviously upset. "Mommy!" she blurted out. "Daddy said a BAD WORD!"

"*Oh, dear,*" thought her mom. "Heaven only *knows* what he said."

"What did he say, Mary Margaret?" she asked, risking the answer.

Eyes wide, Mary Margaret replied, "He said NO!"

Let a pig and a boy have everything they want, and you'll get a good pig and a bad boy.   COPELAND

To know when to be generous and when firm—this is wisdom.   ELBERT HUBBARD

Don't be afraid to tell your children "no."
                                    JOHN K. ROSEMOND
John Rosemond's Six-Point Plan for Raising Happy, Healthy Children

If At First You Don't Succeed ...

Jered, Age 12

As Jered worked on his favorite pastime, origami, the ancient Chinese art of paper folding, he creased the paper over and over, trying unsuccessfully to create the design he had in mind. Utter frustration!

Trying to be helpful, his mom said, "Honey, there's a right way and a wrong way to do it!"

Exasperated, Jered retorted, "Mom, you *know* there's more than one wrong way to do it!"

Failure is only the opportunity to begin again, more intelligently.　　　HENRY FORD

Do not be too timid and squeamish about your actions. All life is an experiment.　　RALPH WALDO EMERSON

Results! Why, man, I have gotten a lot of results. I know several thousand things that won't work.
　　　THOMAS A. EDISON

What Was *That* All About?

Carlos, Age 3

Carlos had really enjoyed visiting his grandparents. When it was time to go home, he threw a fit!

Thrilled with the idea that Carlos wanted to stay, his grandfather decided to have some fun.

"Why don't you want to go?" he asked, egging him on.

Lips quivering, Carlos played his part well in the melodrama.

"'Cause they whip me," he wailed, "for *no* apparent reason!"

The Last One to Know

Kevin, Age 8

As Ms. Lawler, the third-grade teacher, wrote on the chalk board, there were giggles behind her back. They grew louder, too loud to ignore.

"OK, enough!" she said turning to face them. "What's so funny?"

Kevin volunteered. "It's just that when you write on the board, your 'booty' always shakes."

"Kevin!" his teacher scolded, "It is inappropriate for you to say such a thing in front of the class!"

"Well, Ms. Lawler," he said, "everybody already knows it!"

O wad some power the giftie gie us
To see oursel's as ithers see us!   ROBERT BURNS

Things Not Seen

George, Age 5

"Go wash your hands, George," his mom instructed.

"Why?" he whined.

"Because you have germs on them, and dinner is ready."

George headed down the hall, mumbling under his breath. "Germs and Jesus, germs and Jesus ... that's all I ever hear, and I haven't ever seen either one of them!"

The ability to take "leaps of faith" and the willingness to believe and act on "things not seen" form the foundation for some of the most important experiences of life. Spiritual faith ... trust in a relationship ... having a vision ... moving toward goals ... all of these are possible when we open our hearts to believe.

Faith is to believe what we do not see, and the reward of this faith is to see what we believe.
ST. AUGUSTINE

We walk by faith, not by sight.
THE APOSTLE PAUL, II Corinthians 5:7

Fair and Square

Cliff, Age 4

Harlan, Cliff's older brother, was sitting at the kitchen table dreading what lay ahead: preparation for class.

"I hate doing homework," he said. "Why do I have to do it anyway?"

Cliff spoke up. "Harlan," he said, "life is just not fair!"

The only fair in life is a carnival.	UNKNOWN

Filling A Void

Jamie, Age 4

A road crew was busy at work. Their project now complete, they were shoveling dirt back into the excavation.

Jamie observed the operation and said, "Look, Mom, they're taking up a hole!"

Many people would like to "take up" a hole they dug themselves into!

You can't un-ring a bell.	UNKNOWN

Blame Game

Krystal, Age 8

A family friend asked Krystal, "How is school going for you?"

"Pretty good," she answered. "But I am having one problem. I'm working on my science project, and it's not going to be very good."

"I bet it will," she said. "What makes you think it won't?"

Krystal replied, "Because my mom is not very good in science!"

Most of my faults are not my fault!

ASHLEIGH BRILLIANT
Pot-Shots epigrams by Ashleigh Brilliant
of Santa Barbara, CA, appear by special permission

Doesn't Take Much

Cy, Age 4

Cy's parents were excited about the brand new jungle gym set they had bought for his birthday. It had all the bells and whistles, the best that money could buy!

When they took him outside to see it for the first time, his little face fell.

"Gee, Dad," he said, "what I really wanted was a cowboy hat!"

I Beg Your Pardon?

Micah, Age 4

Micah had grown tired of performing his two assigned chores. In a very "sassy" tone, Micah said to his mother, "I always have to set the table and clear the table. I'm tired of doing all the work around here!"

"Micah! You can't talk to me like that!" his mom scolded. "Now go to your room and think about what you did wrong."

A few minutes later, Micah's dad decided to take advantage of a "teachable moment." He talked with Micah at length about the importance of helping out around the house, and of using a nicer tone to express his feelings.

Micah listened wide-eyed. His dad was certain that his lecture had made an impact on the boy.

A short time later, when Micah came back into the living room, his dad prompted, "What do you have to say to your mother?"

Micah said confidently, "Mommy, I forgive you!"

Before you flare up at anyone's faults, take time to count ten . . . ten of your own. UNKNOWN

The Untouchables

Andy, Age 3

Andy was getting ready to go for a swim. His grandmother helped him remove his clothes.

Suddenly self-conscious, he covered himself modestly, and repeated his version of what he had been taught.

With a serious expression, he said, "Nana, we're not ever supposed to let anyone touch our *favorite parts!*"

The favorite parts, as Andy aptly named them, are also the private *parts. Parents need to help their children deal with sexuality, even if they themselves grew up with something less than a healthy perspective.*

Modesty without shame . . . a complex concept, but a worthy goal.

After the Fact

Chad, Age 3

Chad was proud of the progress he had made in learning to say mealtime blessings.

On a weekend family camping trip, his mom handed Chad a plate, and he began to eat. By the time Mom sat down to eat, the boy was finished with his food, and Dad was half through. Suddenly his mom realized that no one had remembered to return thanks.

"Chad, would you like to say the blessing?" she prompted.

"Sure," he said. Bowing his head, he uttered these words:

> "Dear Baby Jesus,
> We ate it all.
> It was good.
>   Amen."

Bless the Lord, O my soul, and all that is within me . . .
                    DAVID, *Psalm 103:1*

Count Me Out

Charles, Age 5

Thirty minutes after the opening bell of the first day of kindergarten, Charles's teacher noticed that he was packing up all of his things and putting them back into his school bag.

"Charles, what are you doing?" she asked.

"I'm going home," he replied.

"You can't go home now! We're going to be here until 2:30 this afternoon."

He looked the teacher squarely in the eye and asked, *"Who signed me up for this?"*

If It Ain't Broke, Don't Break It

A.J., Age 4

A.J.'s mom was in a hurry, a long-established pattern for early mornings! Without thinking, she raised her voice to get A.J.'s attention and to hurry him up.

It caught him off guard, since he was totally immersed in a show on Nickelodeon . . . so much so that he began to cry. Then crying turned to sobbing.

When he could finally speak, he said between sobs, "Mommy . . . you broke . . . my feelings!"

Eternally Grateful

Joshua, Age 5

Joshua's mother was a firm believer: if it's contained, it's controlled . . . a place for everything, and everything in its place. Especially toys.

"Mom, do you know what I'm going to do?" Joshua said, not needing an answer. "Every time I'm done playing with a toy, I'm going to return the toy to the box. Then I'll return the box to the shelf before I get out another toy. And do you know what *you'll* get when I do this?"

"No, Joshua. What will I get?" his mother said.

"You'll get *returnal rewards!*"

Have a place for everything, and then keep the thing somewhere else. This is not a piece of advice, it is merely a custom. MARK TWAIN

Hearing Loss

Kate, Age 5

Having suffered a progressive hearing loss through the years, Kate's grandfather wore hearing aids in both ears. The grandchildren had learned to speak to him slowly and clearly and to allow PopPop to see their faces when they talked.

One evening, Kate had a sudden revelation. "PopPop, I know why you can't hear me," she exclaimed. "You have those plugs in your ears!"

Most conversations are just alternating monologues. The question is, is there any real listening going on?
LEO BUSCAGLIA

To be successful in conversing, try to be more interested *than* interesting.
UNKNOWN

Seek first to understand, then to be understood.
STEPHEN COVEY

Hung Over

Karen, Age 4

It was New Year's Eve ... time to celebrate! At the party, Karen ate several cocktail wieners in a barbecue sauce made with beer.

The next morning, Karen walked into the kitchen, holding her head and moaning, "I think I have an overhang!"

Ebony & Ivory

Dylan, Age 4

Dylan was eagerly awaiting the birth of his first sibling. He told everyone at preschool that he was going to have a baby sister.

Dylan's parents tried for days to get across the idea that it could be a girl *or* a boy. Finally, he seemed to accept it.

But now, he had another question. "Mommy! Mommy! I *know* that you don't know if it's going to be a girl or a boy, but just tell me this . . . will it be black or white?"

Vive La Différence

Charlesy, Age 5

"It won't be long, now, Charlesy and Robert," their dad said. He was referring to the new baby that was on the way.

"I sure hope it's a baby sister," Charlsey stated flatly. "I just don't think I can *take* another boy!"

Wake Me When It's Over

Jill, Age 7
Daughter of Judy Moon Denson

Jill was sleeping soundly when the sun came up. Her mother went in to wake her.

"Jill," she called. No response. "Jill, it's time to get up!" she said, this time pulling on her hand.

"Wait a minute," Jill mumbled into the pillow. "I'm in the middle of a good dream. Let me see what happens."

It doesn't do any harm to dream, providing you get up and hustle once the alarm goes off! UNKNOWN

At A Loss For Words

Bethany, Age 6

Bethany was eavesdropping on her parents' discussion of the day's happenings. Her dad had just delivered Christmas cookies.

"I didn't know exactly what to say to my Jewish clients, so I just said something like 'Enjoy these'," Bethany's dad told her mother.

Bethany piped up, "You should have just given them the cookies and said, 'Happy Harmonica!'"

Oh, well, it's the sentiment that counts . . . a holiday feeling, a giving spirit . . . or is it?

Gloria Estafan sang: "I'd like to say 'I love you,' but the words get in the way." We tend to assume others know how we feel, causing them and us to miss the pleasure of hearing the words and sharing the feelings.

Some words don't come easily. "I'm sorry." "I was wrong." "The truth is, I forgot." "Can you help me?" "I'm afraid." "I appreciate you." "I love you."

It's one thing to regret words that have been said. It's another to regret what was not said, while there was time.

Seeing Spots

Stewart, Age 5

Stewart went for a leisurely drive in the country with his grandmother. They passed a herd of cattle with white and black markings.

"Grandma, look!" he said. "Dalmation cows."

Money Hungry

Kim, Age 6

Kim had grown up hearing a lot of talk about financial matters because her parents owned the local credit bureau.

As the family gathered around the Thanksgiving table, Kim made a pronouncement just as the blessing ended.

"Eat, drink, and be merry," she said, "for tomorrow you may be bankrupt!"

I used to think I was poor. Then they told me I wasn't poor, I was needy. Then they told me it was self defeating to think of myself as needy, I was deprived. Then they told me deprived was a bad image, I was underprivileged. Then they told me underprivileged was overused, I was disadvantaged. I still don't have a dime. But I sure have a great vocabulary.

JULES FEIFFER

I'm living so far beyond my income that we may almost be said to be living apart. HECTOR HUGH MUNRO

Amen to That!

Lindsey, Age 5

Lindsey decided to depart from her usual memorized prayer to say the dinner table "blessing." She said: "Thank you, God, for the plates, the table, the chairs, the napkins, for Mommy and Daddy, for the bread, the meat . . . " She paused, opened one eye to come up with "more material," and spotted the broccoli. She continued, "And that green stuff . . . NO! NO! NO! Not the green stuff! I don't like that. Amen."

> *In general, my children refused to eat anything that hadn't danced on TV.*   ERMA BOMBECK

Amen to That, Too!

Molly, Age 5
Daughter of Judy Moon Denson

Molly's mom, drinking a health drink, complained about its awful taste. Molly's friend, LeeLee asked, "Why are you drinking it, if it's so awful?"

Molly broke in with the explanation.

"Because it's good for you. God makes grossening things because they're good for you."

In One Ear and Out the Other

Bobby, Age 8

Bobby had not been to "big church" very often. When he did go, he found it hard to be quiet. Such was the case when he went to church with his Aunt Opal. Several times during the service, she found it necessary to whisper "helpful" suggestions in his ear.

"Pay attention, Bobby! And listen to the preacher!"

When the service was finally over, Aunt Opal took him home.

"Well, what did the preacher preach about today?" his mother asked.

"I don't know," he said. "I couldn't hear because Aunt Opal kept talking to me!"

Way Back When

Teejay, Age 5

On the way into church one Sunday morning, Teejay asked her dad, "When you were a little boy, was it in the Old Testament or the New Testament?"

Older Than Dirt

Tucker, Age 6
Son of Orley Hood, *The Clarion Ledger*

One morning as Christmas was fast approaching, Tucker found an old Santa Claus hat that belonged to his dad. He wore it all day.

His mom said, "That was Daddy's hat when he was a little boy." Tucker stared in disbelief.

"You mean there was a Santa Claus when Daddy was a boy?"

"Sure," his mom said.

"Santa Claus is older than Daddy?" he asked incredulously. "Mom, how old *is* Santa Claus?"

Better Watch Out

Alex, Age 4

Excitement was building as the holidays approached, and Alex had been rather rambunctious. His mom and dad tried a strategy parents everywhere have used since Ole St. Nick first hit the scene.

"Santa Claus knows everything you do," they warned.

It didn't faze Alex.

So they went a little further.

"He calls your mom and dad and talks to them about whether you're being good!"

That did it! Alex pleaded, "Could you please lie *just once?*"

Alternate Route

Caleb, Age 3

Caleb had popped up out of his seat several times during breakfast to run around the table and "pat" his six-month-old sister, Rebekah, on the head. His mom had hesitated to correct him. He was, after all, expressing affection.

Finally Caleb's mother reached the end of her patience. "Don't come around the table again!" she told Caleb sternly.

Recognizing the seriousness of her tone, he obeyed. This time, rather than running around the table, he climbed on top of it and began to crawl across.

His mom reached across the table, put her hands on his shoulders, and stopped him short.

All at once, Caleb teared up, bowed his head, and reverently said, "*Let us pray!*"

Step By Step

Amy, Age 4
Daughter of Beverly Smallwood

Amy and her mom had let the time slip away as they chatted with Mrs. Franks, the elderly lady who lived on the hill across the street. They quickly said their goodbyes and began the long, winding trek down the driveway. The thick darkness was interrupted only by the distant light of their own carport.

Grasping her mom's hand, Amy exclaimed, "Mommy, Mommy, we can't see!" Seconds later, she made an exciting discovery.

"Oh, look, Mom," she exclaimed, "we can't see out there, but ... if we look down at our feet ... we can see how to take the next step."

Could Your KidSpirational Kid Be in Our Next Book?

KidSpiration... Out of the Mouths of Babes is packed with real stories about real kids. Do you have a favorite story you'd like to submit for our next volume? We'll select the ones that are especially funny, poignant, thought-provoking, or unique.

If you'd like to send us a story, please include the following:

- Child's first name and age at the time of the event;
- The story, giving details that will help us make the story vivid (you may refer to the *KidSpirational Keepsakes Journal* for more complete instructions on how to record the story);
- Your name and relationship to the child;
- Your address, phone, fax, and/or e-mail;
- Your signature.

We'll be excited to read about your *KidSpirational Kid.* Send your story to:

KidSpiration, LLC
Story Submissions
P. O. Box 16414
Hattiesburg, MS 39404

Epilogue

KidSpirational kids! They see life through eyes untainted by the dog-eat-dog mentality, the cynicism, and the polite dishonesty so abundant in the world. Children have quite a talent for cutting sharply and swiftly through the "baloney" and getting right to the meat of the situation, don't they? The adults in their lives are sometimes delighted, sometimes amused, sometimes proud, sometimes mortified by kids' unique and often untimely observations! In reading this book, you've responded to a special invitation into the homes, schools, churches, and automobiles that have provided the stages for these priceless mini-dramas. The stars? They're definitely not actors. They're just kids, real kids, like those in our own lives—being themselves.

Most of us have been entrusted with the opportunity to impact and influence at least one precious child. It is my hope that this book has provided, shall we say, *KidSpiration*—stimulating you to renew your commitment to make a significant difference to the children in your own life. To this end, allow me to offer two important challenges.

First, care enough to *listen*, then *respond* to let the child know that he or she has been heard. I was shaken to the core when one of my teenage clients shared with me a distorted perception from his early childhood. He reported that often, when he had talked to his parents, he had gotten no response. Trying to make sense of this, he actually came to believe that no words were coming from his mouth. While this particular belief is somewhat unusual, it is not at all uncommon for an unnoticed, unheard, unaffirmed child to conclude, "My words, my thoughts, my feelings have no value." It's a short walk from there to "*I have no value.*" Listening—*really* listening—is a beautiful way to communicate to each child, "You matter."

A second way to both affirm the child and preserve treasured family moments is, essentially, to "write a book" on each special child. (You always said you could! And we show you simple how-to's in our *KidSpirational Keepsakes Journal.*)

As Judy Denson and I have spent the last two years talking with parents, grandparents, and teachers, we've become more and more convinced of the importance of preserving in writing the incidents in each child's life. We've heard all too often, "She was a laugh a minute, and I thought I'd never forget the things she said, but right now, I can't remember a one!"

So the challenge is this: Become a scribe for the wee ones who delight and warm your heart! Lewis Carroll said, "Stories are love gifts." What better gift could you offer to a youngster than to journal the stories that capture the evolution of his or her wit, personality, and self expression?

Many years ago, Jesus said, "A little child shall lead them."

"Sh-h-h!" It's happening even now! Do you hear it? It's the song of innocence, the ringing laughter of a child, melodious words from tiny lips. Listen with your heart, and you'll never be the same. You'll experience afresh the beautiful music of hope, of wonder, of joy, and of love!

Dr. Beverly Smallwood

Our kids have so much to tell us.
The question is . . .

About the Authors

Judy Moon Denson discovered early that television was "magical." Never content just to watch, she wanted to be on the inside looking out! And at 14, she was. Her love affair with the small screen now spans four decades—singing, writing, hosting, and producing.

A professional speaker, Judy does keynotes and also enjoys facilitating panel discussions, having both the "skill" for it and the "feel" for it.

She helped launch *The Nashville Network* (TNN) in 1983, appearing nightly on *Nashville Now*.

In 1984, Judy and her husband, Hill, decided to return to Mississippi to have more time with their young daughters. Judy continued to produce segments for TNN, long distance!

Her proudest career moment came in 1985 when she produced and hosted a special saluting the Country Music Associations top award winners: Reba McEntire, Lee Greenwood, and the group ALABAMA.

Her subject matter has broadened since she became a New York Life agent in 1987. (Her most famous client is Brett Favre!) She speaks at industry meetings around the country and was chosen to moderate a session at The Million Dollar Round Table Meeting in 1996, a convention that attracts 5,000 people from 41 countries.

Most recently she co-hosted *Daybreak* on WDAM-TV, garnering a whopping 77% share of the audience!

Judy and family are active members of Parkway Heights United Methodist Church.

(To contact JudyDenson, phone 601-268-7842 or fax 601-268-3467.)

About the Authors

Beverly Smallwood, Ph.D., is a licensed psychologist whose delight with kids began with her own wonderful children, Greg and Amy. Beverly taught elementary school for six years before returning to graduate school in psychology. For the past 20 years, Dr. Smallwood has worked with adults, kids, couples, and families in her psychological practice. Through her clinical work, her writings, and her television appearances, she has equipped literally thousands of people to enrich relationships through meaningful communication, through win-win resolution of conflicts, and through mutual problem-solving.

Further, Beverly works with organizations that want to grow and keep good employees, and with leaders who want to bring out the best in their people. She conducts visioning and strategy sessions, presentations, and workshops, focusing on Leadership, Teamwork, and the Change-Transition Process. She also works one-on-one with leaders, preparing them to become models and coaches of productive teamwork. She has a lineup of training and educational materials designed to support the learning process.

A Professional Member of the National Speakers Association, Beverly has provided programs and seminars for audiences across the United States, Africa, Asia, and Europe. Her client list includes numerous hospitals and other healthcare organizations, Fortune 500 companies, and professional associations.

(To contact Beverly Smallwood, phone 601-264-0890, fax 601-261-0471, or e-mail BevSmallwd@aol.com).

About the Illustrator

Kym Garraway's love for her family, her love for art and her considerable talent have resulted in a thriving business based in her home studio in Mississippi. She produces signed and numbered, limited edition prints, as well as note cards of her watercolor originals. These realistically detailed paintings of florals, fruits, birds, wildlife scenes, and children's themes are in great demand both as individual purchases and as illustrations for various publications.

Her own children, Kayla and Trey, have served as both inspiration and models for much of her work. Their fresh and spontaneous nature are also characteristics of their mother's art.

"Viewing through the eyes of children, it was a delight and a challenge to create illustrations that capture the 'personalities' of these stories."

KYM GARRAWAY

Garraway Originals and Prints
238 West Canebrake Boulevard
Hattiesburg, Mississippi 39402
http://www.nettech-spectrum.com/art

KidSpiration Contributors

Kathleen Adolt
Kate Andrews, Ph.D
Doug Andrews
Judy Aron
Amy Barrett
Tom Barrett
Peggy Bean
Linda Bell
Patricia Bell
Susan I. Bennett
Melnee Berry
Madeline Bingham
Sue Blackmer
Lesa Bostwick
Dorothy Bounds
Wanda Boyles
Patsy S. Bradley
Myra Lee Brasch
Darla Brock
Gail Brown
Carol Brown
Nita Brown
Tucker Buchanan
Jimmy Burkett
Teresa Busalachi
Jerry Clower
Alice Coleman
Susan Comtois
Careme Curry
Jachin Dardar
Clarence Davis
Lori M. Davis
Barbara Brazda Dietze
Michael Dixon
Cynthia L. Dobbins
Sandra Dodd
Carolyn Doolittle
Kathleen Dunn

Frederica Ellis
Celeste Erickson
Opal M. Everitt
Lisa Factor
Kathy Fairleigh
Maxine Felder
Joyce Fetteroll
Amy Ford
Evelyn Fowler
Deanna Frederickson
Lynne Gaines
Jeanne Marie Ganucheau
Kym Garraway
Michael Genrich
Rebecca A. Goodrich
Mr. & Mrs. Kenny Goodwin
Ruth Everitt Gray
Vondell Guthrie
Moshe K. Hadari
Beth Hall
Wilma Hannaford
Ann Hannaford
Gloria Harris
Marlene Harris
Patti Hathaway
Dr. and Mrs. L. E. Hatten
Kathleen Heale
Liz Curtis Higgs
Lynn Hightower
Krista Holloway
Orley Hood
Gena Hopkins
Bill Hudson, Jr.
Billy Hudson, Sr.
Susan Jett
Barbara Bingham Johnson
Lisa Karpowicz
Dorothy Kelly

Jackie & Sonyia Kidd
Regina Kitchens
Salomé R. Kraus
Edward J. Langton
Martha Lawler
Tina Lea
Mary Ann Leavitt
Glenda Leischeidt
Martha Lightsey
Carol Lindley
Dr. & Mrs. Rodney Lovitt
Donna Lussien-Lyne
Laura Magee
Tiffanie Maisel
Ann Mapp
Robert F. Marcum, M.D.
Bill Martin
Charley McCaffrey
David McIlwain
Deborah Mello
Kathleen A. Mertz
Hilda Mims
Barb Mockridge
Cari Morrison
Richard Nelson
Lori A. Nolan
Diane Parker
Marilee Petticrew
Adele Phillips
John D. Pilla
Connie Podesta
Rebecca A. Polk
Gregg Quam
Margaret Rees
Francine Reichman
Kimberle Reinisch
Sandy Riley
Monica Riley
Cavett Robert

Lee Robert
Charles L. Roberts
Sylvia Roberts
Ruth Robinson
Judy Roseberry
Glenna Salsbury, CSP, CPAE
Carmen Sandifer
Kelly Sanner
Margaret Riley Santhanam
Lisa Shelton
Gerrie Shepard
Laura Sosamon
Stephanie Stephens
Judy Sullivan
Chris Sumpter
Donna Sumrall
Kathy Sutton
Leslyn Tamberg
Nanette Taylor
Judy Thacker
Judge Jim Thomas
Charles Thomas
Charles Thomas, Jr.
Amy Van Vranken
Pamela G. Waddle
Gerry Waites
Rachel Walton
Frankie Ward
Christine Webb
Eric Weill
Lezlee Welch
Connie West
Kerri Whitten
Pamela B. White
Susie Wiggins
Martha Kate Wiseman
Donna Rae Woods
Mr. and Mrs. Jeff Yaker
Phyllis Yoder

Listing of Story Titles

References

Brilliant, A. (1994). *I Want to Reach Your Mind: Where Is It Currently Located?* Santa Barbara, CA: Woodbridge Press.

Canfield, J. & Hansen, M.V. (1993). *Chicken Soup for the Soul.* Deerfield Beach, FL: Health Communications, Inc.

Hathaway, P. (1990). *Giving and Receiving Criticism.* Menlo Park, CA: Crisp Publications, Inc.

Hemphill, B. (1992). *Taming the Paper Tiger.* New York: Random House, Inc.

Higgs, L.C. (1995). *Only Angels Can Wing It: The Rest of Us Have to Practice.* Nashville, TN: Thomas Nelson Publishers.

Jewett, C.L. (1982). *Helping Children Cope with Separation and Loss.* Harvard, MA: The Harvard Common Press.

Karnes, F.A. & Bean, S.M. (1993). *Girls and Young Women Leading the Way.* Minneapolis, MN: Free Spirit, Inc.

LeBoeuf, M. (1996). *The Perfect Business.* New York: Simon & Schuster.

Linkletter, A. (1957). *Kids Say the Darndest Things.* Englewood, NJ: Prentice-Hall.

McCarty, O. (1996). *Simple Wisdom for Rich Living.* Atlanta GA: Longstreet Press, Inc.

Podesta, C. & Gatz, J. (1997). *How to be the Person Successful Companies Fight to Keep.* New York: Simon & Schuster.

Rhode, N. (1991). *The Gift of Family.* Nashville, TN: Thomas Nelson Publishers. Available from Smart Practice; 3400 East McDowell Road; Phoenix, AZ 85008.

Rosemond, J.K. (1989). *Six-Point Plan For Raising Happy, Healthy Kids.* Kansas City, MO: Andrews and McMeel.

Salsbury, G. (1995). *The Art of the Fresh Start.* Deerfield Beach, FL: Health Communications, Inc.

Seligman, M.E.P. (1995). *The Optimistic Child.* New York: Houghton Mifflin Company.

KidSpirational Keepsakes

THE JOURNAL

No doubt that as you've read this book, you thought of the many cute, funny, inspiring, thought-provoking things your own children or grandchildren have said. Now, with the guidance of the authors of *KidSpiration*, you too can record those special stories from your own "KidSpirational" kids.

KidSpirational Keepsakes contains helpful suggestions from authors Judy Moon Denson and Beverly Smallwood Ph.D, on how to start and maintain a journal for each child. *KidSpirational Keepsakes* is beautifully bound in a cloth format for durability. It will be used again and again not only when you record your child's words, but also when you read them over and over.

Don't let your little ones grow up without the benefit of recording their childhood in this unique and inspiring way. *KidSpirational Keepsakes* will become a treasured family heirloom.

KidSpirational Keepsakes is available in bookstores and gift shops or can be ordered directly from the publisher by sending $12.95 plus $1.50 postage to:

QUAIL RIDGE PRESS
P. O. Box 123 · Brandon, MS 39043

Credit card orders call toll-free 1-800-343-1583.

KidSpiration: Out of the Mouths of Babes
  ISBN 0-937552-86-0, 5½ x 8½, 208 pages, paperbound, $9.95
KidSpiration Keepsakes: The Journal
  ISBN 0-937552-87-9, 5½ x 8½, 104 pages, clothbound, $12.95

KidSpirational Keynotes

Are you looking for a way to liven up your next meeting? Judy Moon Denson and Dr. Beverly Smallwood can bring the meeting to life with a sensational kickoff, a celebrational closing, or both! The audience is guaranteed to be totally involved, energized, and delighted—they may even be on their feet for a KidSpirational sing-a-long! Their programs, based on stories from the book, can be customized to meet the objectives of the meeting planner. Business groups, parents, grandparents, teachers will find themselves once again looking at life "through the eyes of the youngest among us" in fresh new ways! Judy and Bev may be engaged together or separately—either way, the program is informative and lots of fun!

Judy Denson · 601-268-7842 · Fax 601-268-3467
Beverly Smallwood · 601-264-0890 · Fax 601-261-0471
e-mail BevSmallwd@aol.com

Visit or chat with the authors on the internet at:
www.QuailRidge.com/KidSpiration

Other KidSpiration products are available online or by writing to:
Quail Ridge Press · P. O. Box 123 · Brandon, MS 39043

Or you may call Monday - Friday 8 a.m. to 5 p.m. CST:
1- 800-343-1583

Quail Ridge Press offers a complete line of quality books. Call or write for a free catalog of all Quail Ridge Press publications. Group and volume discounts as well as fundraiser programs are also available upon request.